Osprey Modelling · 23

Modelling Watten-SS Figures

Calvin Tan

Consultant editor Robert Oehler
Series editors Marcus Cowper and Nikolai Bogdanovic

First published in Great Britain in 2005 by Osprey Publishing
Midland House, West Way, Botley, Oxford OX2 0PH, UK
443 Park Avenue South, New York, NY 10016, USA
Email: info@ospreypublishing.com

ISBN 1 84176 837 5

Page layout by Servis Filmsetting Ltd, Manchester, UK
Index by Alan Thatcher
Originated by Solidity Graphics, London, UK
Printed in China through Bookbuilders

05 06 07 08 09   10 9 8 7 6 5 4 3 2 1

A CIP catalogue record for this book is available from the British Library.

FOR A CATALOGUE OF ALL BOOKS PUBLISHED BY OSPREY MILITARY
AND AVIATION PLEASE CONTACT:

NORTH AMERICA
Osprey Direct, 2427 Bond Street, University Park, IL 60466, USA
E-mail: info@ospreydirectusa.com

ALL OTHER REGIONS
Osprey Direct UK, P.O. Box 140 Wellingborough, Northants, NN8 2FA, UK
E-mail: info@ospreydirect.co.uk

www.ospreypublishing.com

Photographic credits

All of the photographs that appear in this work were taken by the
author.

Acknowledgements

The editor and author would like to express their gratitude
to the following companies and organisations, who provided
assistance with and samples of some of the modelling products
that are featured in this work:

Hornet Models
Archer Transfers
New Connections
Aber
Royal Models
The M Workshop
Mig Productions
Vallejo Paints
Nanyang Polytechnic, Singapore

Dedication

To my parents Eddie and Veronica, and my wife Yeh Woey for
their love and support.

Contents

Introduction

Raised to serve as Hitler's personal bodyguards, the Waffen-SS burgeoned from a small militia into a 38-division-strong elite combat unit by the end of World War II. Its men were handpicked according to the dictates of the Aryan ideal; they were imbued with strict discipline and strong political convictions to the Nazi cause. As such, its units were issued with special uniforms and equipped with the most sophisticated weaponry and equipment of the time. In battle, the Waffen-SS would spearhead some of the most pivotal campaigns and key combat operations, proving time after time their right to be called an elite unit, and gaining the respect of even their most hated enemies. Despite their symbiotic association with the Nazi quest for world domination and the acts of racial hatred and genocide that they participated in, to this very day soldiers of the Waffen-SS exert a fascination, particularly for military modellers, wargamers and reenactors.

An SS-Schütze from the 1st SS-Panzer-Division Liebstandarte Adolf Hitler in France 1940. (Stephen Andrew; from Osprey Publishing's Men-at-Arms 401)

An SS-Sturmmann from 1942, carrying an MG34 machine gun, and wearing the reversible camouflage smock. (Stephen Andrew; from Osprey Publishing's Men-at-Arms 401)

Apart from the evocative historical appeal of such a topic, many modellers are drawn to the aesthetic details of Waffen-SS uniforms. Its divisions pioneered the deployment of camouflage clothing on a large scale, and made use of numerous exotic patterns in the plentiful types of standard and non-standard uniforms and field wear.

In response, many figure and model kit manufacturers have satisfied the demand for this popular subject with frequent releases of Waffen-SS figures, making it one of the most widely available subjects on the modelling market. Furthermore, the emergence of numerous websites, photo-journals and publications over the years has, in parallel, increased the accessibility of reference materials.

However, representing camouflage patterns in 1/35-scale modelling is no easy task, and it's with this in mind that this book was written and prepared. One of my key aims is to assist the modeller in tackling some of the most technically demanding aspects of figure painting. Embarking with the use of acrylic paints (a medium that's fast gaining popularity amongst many modellers today) this book will also feature useful tips, techniques, colour plates and after-market products to improve stock figures, or to create an accurate scale representation of a Waffen-SS soldier. The builds will essentially focus more on techniques for problem solving rather than just direct finishing methods. Additional tips on design concepts and groundwork techniques will also be provided for the reader, with the aim of reinforcing my holistic approach towards creating what can hopefully be termed a miniature work of art.

Finally, given the potentially controversial nature of the Waffen-SS, I would like to stress that this book is quintessentially a guidebook to aid the modeller in rendering this historical subject in scale form. In no way does it seek to glorify Nazi politics or practices. I hope that you will enjoy the work and that some of the techniques and tips will prove useful in your future modelling endeavours.

SS-Sturmmann, 1st SS-Panzer-Division 'Leibstandarte Adolf Hitler', Kursk, 1943

Subject:	SS-Sturmmann, 1st SS-Panzer-Division *'Leibstandarte Adolf Hitler', Kursk, 1943*
Project overview:	Painting a camouflage smock with acrylic paints, coupled with some simple techniques to improve a stock white metal figure.
Modeller:	Calvin Tan
Skill level:	Intermediate
Base kit:	Hornet Models (GH02)
Scale:	1/35
Additional detailing sets used:	Tamiya 35204 German Infantry Weapons Set A (Early/Mid WWII) Royal Models German Army Equipment (RM-203) Aber German Panzer Troop Accessories (PE 35A86) Dry transfers: Archer Transfers SS Uniform Patches (FG35042A)
Tools and materials:	M-Tools MT 25018 Diamond File Gunze Sanyo GNZB 517 – Mr. Resin Primer Spray
Paints:	Vallejo Model Colour: German Camouflage Beige WWII 821, German Camouflage Pale Brown 825, SS Camouflage Bright Green 833, Salmon Rose 835, Sunny Skin Tone 845, Leather Brown 871, US Field Drab 873, Beige Brown 875, Reflective Green 890, Dark Prussian 899, English Uniform 921, Russian Uniform 924, Black 950, White 951, Military Green 975, Flat Brown 984, Deck Tan 986. Humbrol enamels: Super Silver 11, Flat Black 33, Khaki Drill 72. Gunze Sanyo lacquer-based paints: Flat Black 33, Character Yellow 109. Winsor & Newton oil paints: Prussian Blue, Raw Umber. Daler Rowney acrylic artists ink: Sepia.

Introduction

Acrylic paints are a relatively new development in the field of visual arts, but it has not taken long for military modellers to find uses for them. In recent years, many modellers have gradually made the switch to acrylic paints in lieu of traditional mediums like oils and enamels. Made by binding pigments in synthetic polymer emulsified by water, they are, in short, water-soluble liquid plastic paints. They possess good adhesive qualities; are stable (meaning that the pigments will not separate easily from the binder); resist oxidation, fungus, decomposition; and will not yellow or fade over time. This medium proves especially favourable to me; in the humidity of South-East Asia, where I live, oil paints are more susceptible to fungus growth and decomposition. Furthermore, being water soluble, the clean up process is very convenient and reduces the need to use hazardous solvents.

However, despite their many attributes, acrylic paints are not without their drawbacks. Being a water-based medium, they dry rapidly – which is both an advantage and disadvantage. The time it takes for water to evaporate is the time it takes for these paints to dry. Thus the modeller has little time to manipulate the paint once it has been applied to the surface of the model.

Conversely, the advantage of a fast drying time is that the modeller can apply many layers of paint in a short amount of time. Modellers can very effectively employ glazing and layering techniques when using acrylics. Corrections can also be executed almost immediately, as the layers of paint bind to one another very well because of their good adhesive qualities.

Painting camouflage patterns

Before embarking on painting a uniform, it's vital to study the design of the camouflage pattern. Bear in mind that the patterns throughout are repetitive and this is particularly useful in deciphering the more complex designs by looking for recurring forms. Understanding the design will also enable you to determine the placement of the colour patterns in relation to how light falls on the figure. Shading a figure in camouflage uniform often presents a perplexing problem to most modellers, but by employing a little artistic licence now and then this problem can be overcome. Below are some key tips that I would like to share with you.

- Use the pattern to tone the figure. Start by identifying the darkest or lightest colours in the camouflage pattern and learn to place them towards the shaded or highlighted areas respectively.
- Understand the printing process of the pattern. This determines the order of colours to be painted. More often than not it's the darker colour which is overlaid onto a lighter one, due to the properties of fabric dyes.
- To better visualise the pattern, think of it as a sort of 'ocean map'. The larger areas will be your large land masses, and the smaller spots will be your islands. Work out the positions of the 'large land masses' first and use them to place the 'islands' in between. You may position the darker 'large land masses' towards the shadow areas to enhance the shadows or vice versa for the lighter 'large land masses'.

Preparation and detailing

The figure chosen was Hornet Models GH02, with its fine rendition of drapes, anatomy and pose. Finer details and equipment, however, such as the belt buckle bayonet were not well reproduced and had to be scraped away with a scalpel. The buckle bayonet was replaced with a photo-etch offering from Royal Models RM203 German Army Equipment (Infantry Equipment) and Tamiya ITEM 35205 German Infantry Equipment Set B (Mid/Late WW2) respectively. The bayonet was a relatively fragile detail and was removed to prevent breakage as the modelling of the other features continued. Pitting on the metal surface was filled with Gunze Sanyo Surfacer 500.

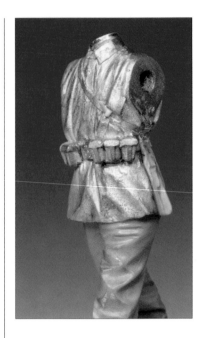

1. A small buckle on the carrying strap of the gas mask canister was omitted from the original model. This was sculpted with epoxy putty by first creating a square bulge for the strap and allowing it to set completely.

2. Next the buckle is recreated with a strip of thinly rolled epoxy putty placed around the square bulge, with the aid of a fine tipped brush moistened with Gunze Sanyo Thinner.

3. The kit's gas mask canister and entrenching tool were discarded and the cavity in its place was filled with epoxy putty.

4. More accurate versions of the entrenching tool and modified gas mask canisters came from Tamiya No. 35205 German Infantry Equipment Set B (Mid/Late WW2). They were embedded into the soft putty to obtain a more natural 'sit'. The skirting for the camouflage smock was re-sculpted with the aid of a needle and brush moistened with Gunze Sanyo Thinner.

5. The entrenching tool and gas mask canister were then removed from the putty. The direction of the carrying straps for the gas mask canister was also changed by filing away the original strap from the right shoulder and filling the creases with epoxy putty.

6. The original water bottle was also removed from the bread bag and holes were drilled in to provide anchor points for the replacement mess tin and canteen.

7. To achieve a more natural sit, a thin layer of putty was first applied over the bread bag.

8. Next, the replacement mess tin and canteen from Tamiya (No. 35204 German Infantry Equipment Set A, Early/Mid WW2) were embedded into the soft putty before it set completely. The retaining set on the mess tin was made from paper stiffened with superglue, and the buckle fashioned from epoxy putty.

9. The canvas belt loop straps and the belt hooks of the bread bag were fashioned from strips of thinly rolled sheets of epoxy putty, attached with a moist brush.

10. When set, superficial details like the buttons, D rings and canteen retaining strap were applied and fashioned with a brush moistened with Gunze Sanyo Thinner.

11. A wire was inserted through a hole drilled through the arms and into the torso to enable a more secure fit.

12. The hole on the side of the arm was patched with epoxy putty and the kit's rifle removed with a scalpel and diamond file from M Tools.

13. The figure's thumb was removed and cavities were filled with epoxy putty.

14. Prior to setting, a replacement rifle from Tamiya (No. 35204 German Infantry Equipment Set A, Early/Mid WW2) was embedded into the epoxy putty to attain a more natural 'sit'. Note the new thumb modelled from epoxy putty.

15. The left hand holding the Teller Mine 43, from Hornet Models (HM-HANDS02), was hollowed out with a 0.5mm drill bit to accommodate the carrying handle.

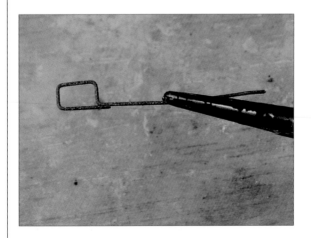

16. The carrying handle was made from fuse wire.

17. The carrying handle attached to the Teller Mine 43 from Dragon Models (6058 German Panzerjäger, Eastern Front 1944).

18. The completed figure ready for priming.

19. Another view of the completed figure prior to priming.

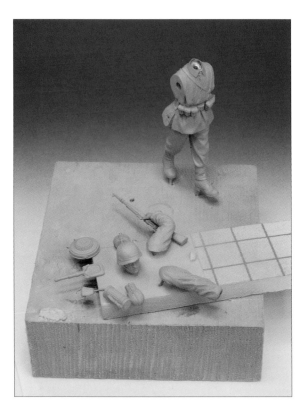

20. To facilitate the painting process, parts such as the head, upper limbs and equipment were broken down into sub-assemblies and primed with Gunze Sanyo Resin Primer.

21. The groundwork was built up from epoxy putty and covered with a mix of dried roots, static grass, and fine gravel. The figure was bedded in to obtain a comfortable fit before the putty had completely set.

Detailing the gas mask canister

22. The circular rings forming the disc and lip on the base of the canister were modelled with a thin strip of epoxy putty wrapped around a smooth jeweller's metal burnisher. Apply a small amount of Vaseline to the burnisher to prevent the ring of putty from attaching to the metal surface, and to allow it to slide off easily when cured.

23. The ring forming the lip of the base was transferred with the aid of a moist, pointed brush to the base of the Tamiya gas canister.

24. The outer lip and inner ring were set with Tamiya Extra Thin Cement applied with a fine-tipped brush.

25. The inner disc of the lid on the canister was created by embedding a circular disc from Aber.

26. Once set in place, the inner diameter for the outer rim was measured with a pair of dividers.

27. The outer rim was created in the same fashion as the rings forming the outer lip of the base, and secured with Tamiya Extra Fine Cement.

28. The completed upper lid.

29. The closure clip was first modelled with a thin strip of putty.

30. Next, secondary details were fashioned with the aid of a brush, a needle, and a sharp scalpel.

31. Final details, such as the hinge and closure stud, were modelled with bits of putty, and the pull tab was fashioned from a thin strip of putty.

Painting the figure

32. RIGHT Paint containers can be improvised from inverted 35mm film canisters secured to a piece of adhesive-backed foam board. They can also be resealed after each painting session, saving the time and effort of mixing new batches of paints.

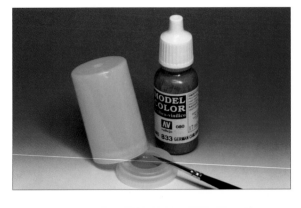

33. BELOW RIGHT Sub-assemblies and accessories were mounted on an adhesive-backed piece of compressed foam for easy painting.

34. BELOW The whole figure was primed in Gunze Sanyo Flat Black.

The face

35. The face was dry-brushed with Vallejo White 951.

36. The face was then dry-brushed with a base colour consisting of a 50/50 mix of Sunny Skin Tone 845 and Salmon Rose 835.

37. Next, a light wash of a mid tone (consisting of a 2:2:1:5 mix of English Uniform 921, Flat Brown 984, Vermilion 909 and the base colour respectively) was applied to subdue the harsh shadows.

38. Next, the high points of the base colour were glazed over to recapture the contrast.

39. An intermediate highlight colour was created by adding a small amount of white to the base colour.

40. Final highlights, consisting of a higher proportion of white added to the base colour, were glazed onto the high points to further accentuate them.

41. The deep shadow colour, consisting of a mix of 3:7 of Vermillion 909 to Black respectively, was carefully glazed into the deep recesses of the features. The whites of the eyes were painted with the final highlight colour whereas the colour for the lips was obtained by mixing Flat Brown 984, Vermilion 909 and Base Colour in a ratio of 3:1:6 respectively.

42. The completed face with the final highlights and details painted in. The iris was painted with Dark Prussian Blue 899 mixed with a small amount of Black 950, with the sparkle in the centre 'borrowed' from the same colour as the final highlight. The unshaven look was created by a thin layer of Raw Umber oil paint.

The camouflage smock (Tarnjacken) in Plane Tree Pattern No. 5

43. The superficial details of the camouflage smock were brought out by a light dry-brushing of Vallejo White 951.

44. The base colour of the Plane Tree pattern smock was created with a 9:1 mix of Vallejo German Camouflage Pale Brown 825 and Flat Brown 984. This was dry-brushed over the white dry-brushing, forming the first level of shade and highlight for the camouflage pattern.

45. The harsh effects of the dry-brushing were subdued with a wash consisting of a 1:4 mix of Black to the base colour.

46. Vallejo Military Green 975 was painted on with a 00 brush to represent the 'large land masses and the islands' of medium green.

47. The lighter shade of green was formed with 2:3:1 mix of Sunny Skin Tone 845, SS Camouflage Bright Green 833, and Military Green 975 respectively, and carefully applied within the 'large land masses' of medium green.

48. The pattern was completed with the dark green 'large land masses and islands' consisting of a 2:1 mix of Military Green 975 and Black 950.

49. The camouflage pattern receives more definition with a 000 brush, and a thin glaze of Daler Rowney Sepia ink was applied to the shadows of the folds.

50. The seams of the smock were outlined with glazes of Sepia ink mixed with Vallejo Black 950.

51. The highlight colours were prepared by mixing a small amount of Sunny Skin Tone 845 into the base colours of each colour shade. These were thinned down to a milk-like consistency and applied to the high points of the smock in successive layers.

52. ABOVE LEFT The mess tin and canteen cup were undercoated with Gunze Sanyo lacquer based Silver 8.

53. ABOVE These were then painted over with Black and dry-brushed with Military Green 975.

54. LEFT Both items were soaked in water for approximately 30 minutes to loosen the acrylic overcoat, before scraping the top layer away with a sharp scalpel blade to reveal the silver undercoat.

55. The base colour of the 'Keilhose' combat trousers was created with a 2:1 mix of Extra Dark Green 896 and Field Grey 830. Highlight colours were formed by mixing various quantities of US Field Drab 873 and German Camouflage Beige 821 into the base colour. The leather parts were glazed with successive layers of Sepia ink to provide a leathery sheen. The edges were then defined with Leather Brown 871. The buckle was painted with a mix of Humbrol Super Silver, Raw Umber, and Prussian Blue oil paint. Highlighting on the high points was done with a little Humbrol Khaki Drill 72 mixed with Super Silver 11 to subdue the shine of the aluminium surface.

56. Russian Uniform 924 was used as the base colour of the bread bag. Highlighting and edging was done with incremental amounts of German Camouflage Beige 821 and Khaki 988 added to the base colour. The seams of the reinforced panel of the trouser seat were outlined with a glaze of black paint.

57. The felt texture of the canteen cover was replicated by stippling US Field Drab 873 over a base colour mixed from Beige Brown 875 and Olive Drab 889.

58. The back of the completed 'Keilhose' trousers.

59. The rifle sling together with the buckle was created from a thin strip of paper stiffened with superglue.

60. It was secured to the looped end of the noose and trimmed with a sharp blade.

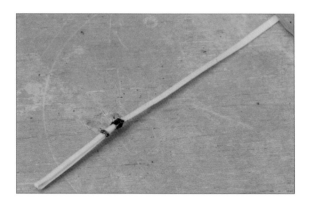

61. The completed rifle sling with the retaining loop.

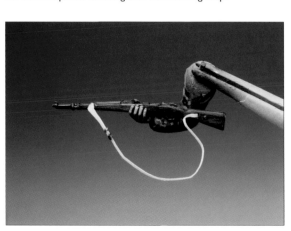

62. The metal parts of the Kar98 Rifle were dry-brushed with Humbrol Super Silver 11 and burnished with graphite powder. The grain of the wooden stock was painted with a series of successive glazes of Leather Brown 871, Flat Brown 984 and Sepia ink.

63. The gas mask canister was secured to the figure with its carrying strap made from paper stiffened with superglue. The right arm was secured to the figure with superglue.

64. The canister was painted with Military Green 975, Black 950 and US Field Drab 873. The pull tab and carrying strap were painted with varying proportions of colours used for the bread bag. Corrections to the fit of the arms were made with small bits of epoxy putty feathered into the cavities.

65. The corrected parts were given an undercoat of Gunze Sanyo lacquer based Flat Black.

66. The camouflage pattern on the sleeves was painted, shaded and highlighted. The shirt collar was painted using the same colour as the trousers with the seams outlined with Sepia ink and black paint.

67. The runic collar tabs (*Kragenpatte*) came from Archer Transfers FG35042A SS Uniform Patches. They were first transferred to a small piece of double-sided tape for added relief and trimmed to size before being picked up with the side of a sharp blade and slid onto the collar with the aid of a dry brush.

Colour chart no. 1: Plane Tree Pattern

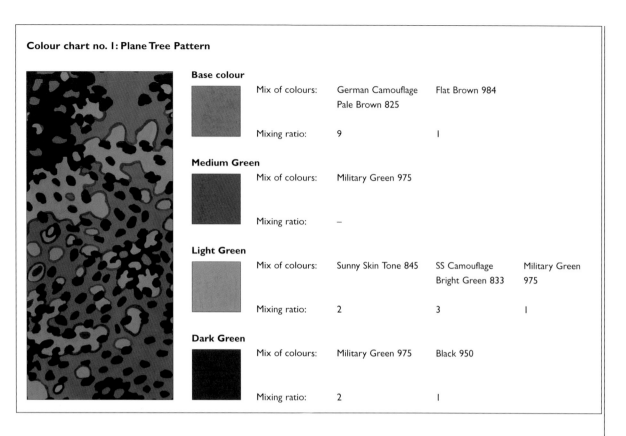

Base colour

Mix of colours:	German Camouflage Pale Brown 825	Flat Brown 984	
Mixing ratio:	9	1	

Medium Green

Mix of colours:	Military Green 975
Mixing ratio:	–

Light Green

Mix of colours:	Sunny Skin Tone 845	SS Camouflage Bright Green 833	Military Green 975
Mixing ratio:	2	3	1

Dark Green

Mix of colours:	Military Green 975 · Black 950
Mixing ratio:	2 · 1

The groundwork

68. The groundwork was first painted over with Humbrol Flat Black 33.

69. Next it was dry-brushed with German Camouflage Beige 821.

70. A wash consisting of a 1:1 mix of US Field Drab 873 and Black 950 was applied.

71. Another wash consisting of 3:3:1 mix of US Field Drab 873, German Camouflage Beige 821, and Tamiya Flat Base X-21 was applied immediately and allowed to 'mingle' with the first wash.

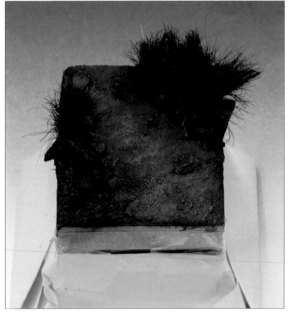

72. This process was repeated with the first and second wash with varying quantities of Field Drab, Beige and Black until the desired effect was obtained. Note that the soft, dusty effect was achieved by adding Tamiya Flat Base X-21 into the wash. Both the long and short grass came from Woodland Scenics FG171 Field Grass-Natural Straw and FL63 Flock-Light Green respectively.

73. The grass was air-brushed with a 1:4 mix of Gunze Sanyo lacquer based Flat Black 33 and Character Yellow 109.

74. The grass was highlighted with a dry-brush colour of Reflective Green 890 and SS Camouflage Bright Green 833. Additional highlights to the dirt trail were added with more successive washes of US Field Drab 873, German Camouflage Beige 821, and Deck Tan 986 in varying quantities and mixes.

75. The figure was attached to the groundwork for the last leg of the painting process so as to ensure overall colour coordination. Leggings were painted with Khaki 988. The leather fasteners were glazed with Sepia and highlighted with varying amounts of Leather Brown 871 and German Camouflage Beige 821. Highlights of the boots were brought out with the groundwork colour of US Field Drab 873, German Camouflage Beige 821 and Deck Tan 986, whereas glazes of Black 950 were used to accentuate the shadows and outlines of the seams.

Finishing

76. The helmet cover (*Stahlhelmbezüge*) was painted; the rocker clip was modelled from a small strip of epoxy putty and attached with a brush moistened with Gunze Sanyo Thinner.

77. The Teller Mine 43 was painted with a 3:1:1 base mix of Military Green 975, Black 950, and US Field Drab 873. A small amount of German Camouflage Beige 821 was added to the base mix and applied in thin successive glazes to create the band of highlight on the edges of the mine.

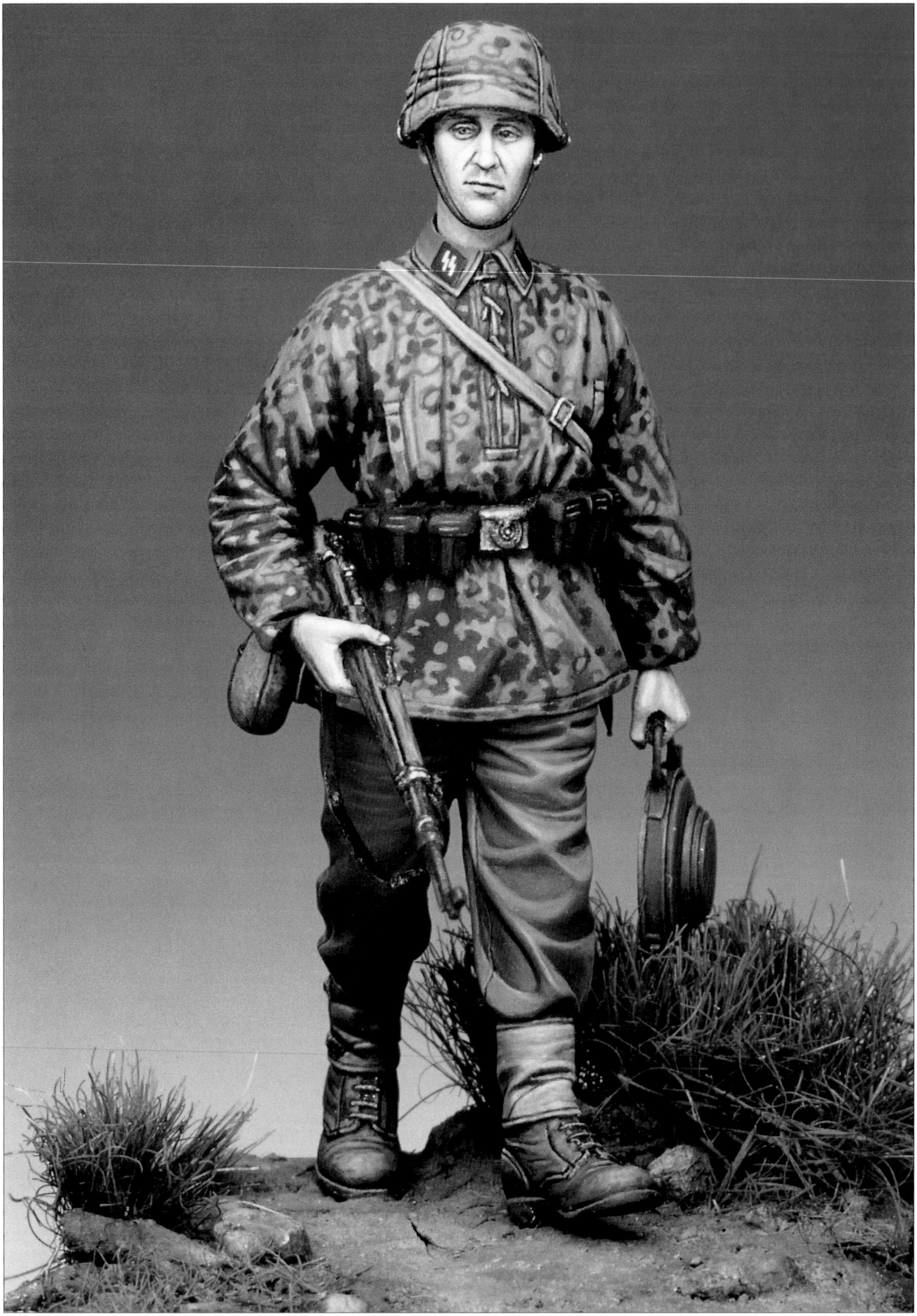

ABOVE AND OPPOSITE PAGE **The completed figure and base.**

A rear view of the completed figure, showing the equipment in detail.

A close-up of the groundwork showing the details on the boots and leggings.

SS-Scharführer, 1st SS-Panzer-Division 'Leibstandarte Adolf Hitler', Normandy, 1944

Subject:	SS-Scharführer, 1st SS-Panzer-Division 'Leibstandarte Adolf Hitler', Normandy, 1944
Project overview:	Converting a tank crew in overalls to a Panzer wrap tunic (Panzerjacke) and painting the 'dot pattern' camouflage.
Modeller:	Calvin Tan
Skill level:	Intermediate
Base kit:	Hornet Models (GH13)
Scale:	1/35
Additional detailing sets used:	Tamiya 35204 German Infantry Weapons Set A (Early/Mid WWII) Royal Models German Army Equipment (RM-203) Aber German Panzer Troop Accessories (PE 35A86) Aber Ammo Bottom Plates for German 88mm and 75mm (PE 35A48) Scale Link Leaves-Elm/Beech (SLF039) Dry transfers: Archer Transfers Heer Shoulder Boards for Panzer Crews (FG35043B); SS Uniform Patches (FG35042A).
Paints:	Vallejo Model Colour: German Camouflage Beige WWII 821, German Camouflage Black Brown 822, German Camouflage Orange Ochre 824, SS Camouflage Bright Green 833, Salmon Rose 835, Sunny Skin Tone 845, Black Grey 862, US Field Drab 873, Beige Brown 875, Tan Yellow 912, Yellow Ochre 913, English Uniform 921, Black 950, White 951, Military Green 975, Orange Brown 981. Humbrol enamels: Super Silver 11, Flat Black 33, Khaki Drill 72. Gunze Sanyo lacquer-based paints: Flat Black 33, Character Yellow 109. Winsor & Newton oil paints: Prussian Blue, Raw Umber. Daler Rowney acrylic artists ink: Sepia.

Introduction

The tank battles of the Normandy campaign have long been a fertile source of inspiration and interest for World War II AFV and diorama modellers. Legendary names, such as Michael Wittmann and Ernst Barkmann, have almost become synonymous with the Tiger and Panther tanks, and have long galvanized the imagination of Axis armour aficionados into creating their own renditions of these powerful war machines. As plastic model manufacturers churn out every known variant of popular Allied and Allied armour, an even greater number of tank crews and tank riders are being produced to compliment each new release.

Despite the convenience of breaking into a pack of resin or plastic figures and swapping some limbs and heads to attain the desired result, stock parts still present some limitations to fully articulating one's artistic requirements. Falling short of fully sculpting your own figures, conversions can be made to existing figures with some minor sculpting. I highly recommend builds in this vein to anyone who aspires to sculpt his own figure one day; you can learn a lot from recreating the features and details of a good base sculpture.

Converting the figure

1. To begin, it's very important to select a base figure endowed with a good anatomical representation of the final pose. I chose to base mine on Hornet models GH13, as it had the desired pose and qualities of form required.

2. The details on the chest of the overalls were scraped away with a sharp blade and embedded into a lump of Blue-Tac before filing to shape with a diamond file. These files are ideal for such tasks, as they do not clog with grit, unlike the conventional steel ones.

3. The trousers of the overalls were too baggy to represent the Panzer trousers (*Panzerhose*). The form had to be filed down with a conic diamond blur attached to a pin vice, using the original crease and drapes as guides.

4. Scuff marks on the filed-down areas were given a light rub of steel wool.

5. The arm was secured with a braided piece of wire inserted through a hole drilled through at the shoulder.

6. A rough shape of the right hand modelled from Blue-Tac was placed at the hip to determine the position of the right arm. The joints on the limbs and head were frozen with epoxy putty once the pose had been finalised.

7. The right hand and a new neck were modelled from epoxy putty.

8. The right arm was temporarily removed and the collars for the inner tunic were built up with epoxy putty. Discs from Aber PE 35A86 German Panzer Troop Accessories were temporarily attached to the collars to give a quick mark out of the headphones position.

9. The headphones from my spares box were attached to the putty and the collar openings were modelled with thinly rolled sheets of epoxy putty.

10. The creases and collar openings of the Panzer tunic were further refined by attaching narrow 'sausages' of epoxy putty.

11. They were blended together with a pointed brush moistened with Gunze Sanyo Thinner.

12. The collar, tunic flap and binoculars strap were next modelled from rolled putty attached with a moistened brush. Two holes drilled into the front of the chest provided the anchor points for the binoculars.

13. The seams along the edge of the collar and tunic flap were made with a sharp blade when the putty had cured to a semi-hardened state (approximately one hour at 26 degrees Celsius room temperature). When completely set, surface imperfections were smoothed out with sandpaper, and the binoculars from 35204 German Infantry Weapons Set A (Early/Mid WWII) were attached to the figure. Deeper creases along the upper right thigh where the leg crosses were defined with a No.15 Swann Morton scalpel and later refined with steel wool.

14. Modelling of the tunic flap continued with rolled putty, starting from the collar openings. The Knight's Cross and Tank Assault Badge from PE 35A86 German Panzer Troop Accessories were embedded into the soft putty for a comfortable fit.

15. The preliminary form of the M40 overseas cap (Feldmütze neuer Art) and collar now began to take shape. The trouser fly was modelled from a thin strip of rolled putty. The seams on the overseas cap and remaining collar were carefully pressed in with a scalpel blade.

16. The *Totenkopf* (Death's Head) and eagle emblem, from Royal Models RM-203 German Army Equipment (Infantry Equipment), were pressed into the soft putty prior to setting.

17. The hair was modelled and textured with a stiff brush. The upper lip of the overseas cap was built up with a thin strip of rolled putty. The watch pocket was formed from rolled putty.

18. The necessary corrections to the form were made with bits of putty feathered in with a thinner-moistened brush. The watch pocket was refined and detailed with a scalpel blade and thinner-moistened brush.

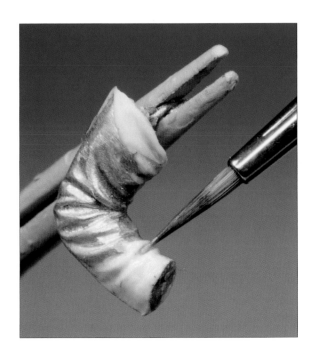

19. The tunic sleeves were modified with putty and the creases 'painted' out with a 00 pointed brush.

20. This was left to cure to a semi-hardened state before the seams were pressed in with a scalpel blade.

21. The ammunition crates used as the backdrop came from Tamiya 35188 German Tank Ammo-Loading Crew. A section of fuse wire inserted into a hole made with a 0.5mm drill bit provided the anchor point for the left hand.

22. It was then coated with epoxy putty, with the general form blocked out with a pair of tweezers and brush.

23. The individual fingers were divided with a scalpel blade and trimmed to size.

24. The digits were loosely shaped with both a fine-tipped brush and sewing needle dipped in petroleum jelly (Vaseline), and allowed to set completely.

25. The digits were further shaped and refined with a scalpel blade.

26. ABOVE A final sanding with a conic diamond bit and 400-grit sandpaper completed the sculpting process.

27. RIGHT The upper limbs were attached to the figure, and the ammunition crate was propped up with Blue-Tac for a test fit.

28. Superficial details, like the seams on the back and sleeves of the tunic, were made from thinly sliced strips of rolled putty and applied with a thinner-moistened brush.

29. These were left to set for approximately 10 minutes before the excess was removed with a scalpel blade.

30. The binocular buttoning strap was made from strips of thinly rolled putty shaped with a moist brush.

31. The completed figure, with a photo-etched buckle added from Royal Models RM-203 German Army Equipment (Infantry Equipment). A thin glaze of Gunze Sanyo Resin Primer was applied over the converted areas to correct superficial imperfections.

32. The figure was primed with Gunze Sanyo Resin Primer and test fitted to the groundwork.

33. Static grass from FL63 Flock-Light Green was added.

Painting the Dot/Pea Pattern camouflage

34. The whole figure was undercoated with Gunze Sanyo Flat Black.

35. I began painting the pattern from the back as I had intended to paint the front of the uniform together with the groundwork for better overall colour synchronisation. White 951 was dry-brushed over the black undercoat prior to another dry-brush of the base colour consisting of a 5:1:1 mix of 873 US Field Drab, 921 English Uniform, and 822 German Camouflage Black Brown respectively. This is to enhance the chroma or the quality of a colour, that is, the combination of hue and brightness of subsequent colour, as well as a preliminary establishment of highlights and shadows.

36. The harsh effects of dry-brushing were mitigated with successive washes of the base colour mixed with varying quantities of Sepia ink for a smooth finish.

37. The base colour was shaded and highlighted by varying the mixtures of 822 German Camouflage Black Brown/Sepia ink and 845 Sunny Skin Tone into the base colour applied in successive washes. Contrary to the perception that the Pea Pattern consists of just dots, there are two colours of 'large land masses', namely sand/pink and dark green, that form the design of the pattern. I decided to lay down the 'large land masses' of Dark Green made up of a 2:1 mix of Military Green 975 and Black 950 applied with a 00 brush from Windsor & Newton Series 7.

38. The sand/pink 'large land masses and islands', consisting of a 3:4:1 mix of Sunny Skin Tone 845, Salmon Rose 835, and 921 English Uniform, were painted on.

39. Reflective Green 890 made up the medium green spots, whereas the light green spots consisted of a 3:5:1 mix of Sunny Skin Tone 845 Camouflage Bright Green 833 and Military Green 975.

40. The dark green and base colour spots were next painted on.

41. The shadows were defined with a light wash of Sepia ink.

42. A light glaze of Yellow Ochre 913 was applied to the highlights of the creases for a more muted result. The process of outlining with Sepia ink and edging with Sunny Skin Tone 845 completed the rendering process for the back of the figure.

43. The wooden texture of the ammunition crates was recreated with successive glazes of Tan Yellow 912, German Camouflage Beige WWII 821, and US Field Drab 873.

44. The figure was attached to the groundwork, and painting the front of the figure was resumed.

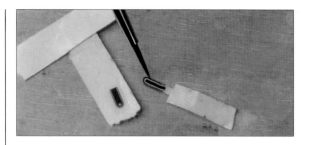

45. To make the shoulder boards, I attached transfers from Archer Transfers FG35043B Heer Shoulder Boards for Panzer Crews to two plies of double-sided tape. This gave the required thickness for the boards at 1/35 scale. I proceeded to trim the shape with a sharp blade, and painted red and white stripes to denote the service arm and rank respectively.

47. The connection wire was made from sewing thread, frayed into two parts and stiffened with superglue.

46. I carefully transferred the shoulder boards onto the *Panzerjacke*. I glazed a thin line of Salmon Rose 835 over the red stripes to represent the service arm of armoured forces. The eagle patch on the left shoulder was made using the same method as the collar tabs described in the previous chapter. The head band connecting the headphones together came from Aber PE 35A86 German Panzer Troop Accessories with the swivel rocker brackets made from a thin strip of epoxy putty. The pair of binoculars came from Tamiya 35204 German Infantry Weapons Set A (Early/Mid WWII), and were undercoated with a 3:1 mix of English Uniform 921 and Black 950.

48. The headphones and left hands were attached at respective ends and undercoated with Black 950. The inner tunic was painted with 862 Black Grey rendered with mixes of Black and 845 Sunny Skin Tone. The binoculars were painted in German Camouflage Orange Ochre 824, highlighted and edged with mixes of German Camouflage Beige WWII 821, and outlined with Sepia.

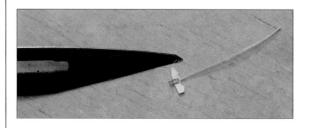

49. The two-pronged plug was made from fuse wire and thread attached to a small strip of paper.

50. The strip was folded into one, stiffened with superglue, and filed to shape with a diamond file.

52. The base of the empty cartridges from Tamiya 35189 Tiger I Brass 88mm Projectiles were sanded down with a diamond file and fitted with base plates from Aber PE 35A48 Ammo Bottom Plates for German 88mm and 75mm. Seams were patched with a lacquer-based gold paint from a felt-tip permanent marker, applied with a 00 brush.

51. It was attached to the left hand, undercoated with Black 950, and painted with Beige Brown 875. The overseas cap was rendered with Black 950 mixed with varying proportions of Sunny Skin Tone 845 and Beige Brown 875.

53. To make the shrubs, I stacked two frets of photo-etched leaves and braided them together.

54. I then proceeded to texture the stems with Gunze Sanyo Resin Primer applied using a fine-tipped brush.

55. I bent and twisted each leaf to the side for a more natural looking finish.

56. Next I airbrushed the shrubs with Gunze Sanyo Flat Black. I rendered them with varying mixes of 833 German Camouflage Bright Green, Orange Brown 981, Military Green 975 and Sunny Skin Tone 845 for the leaves, and washes of German Camouflage Black Brown 822 and Sap Green ink for the stems. Flat Black was also airbrushed along the lip of the cartridge to simulate the gunpowder soot.

ABOVE, BELOW, AND OPPOSITE PAGE **The completed figure.**

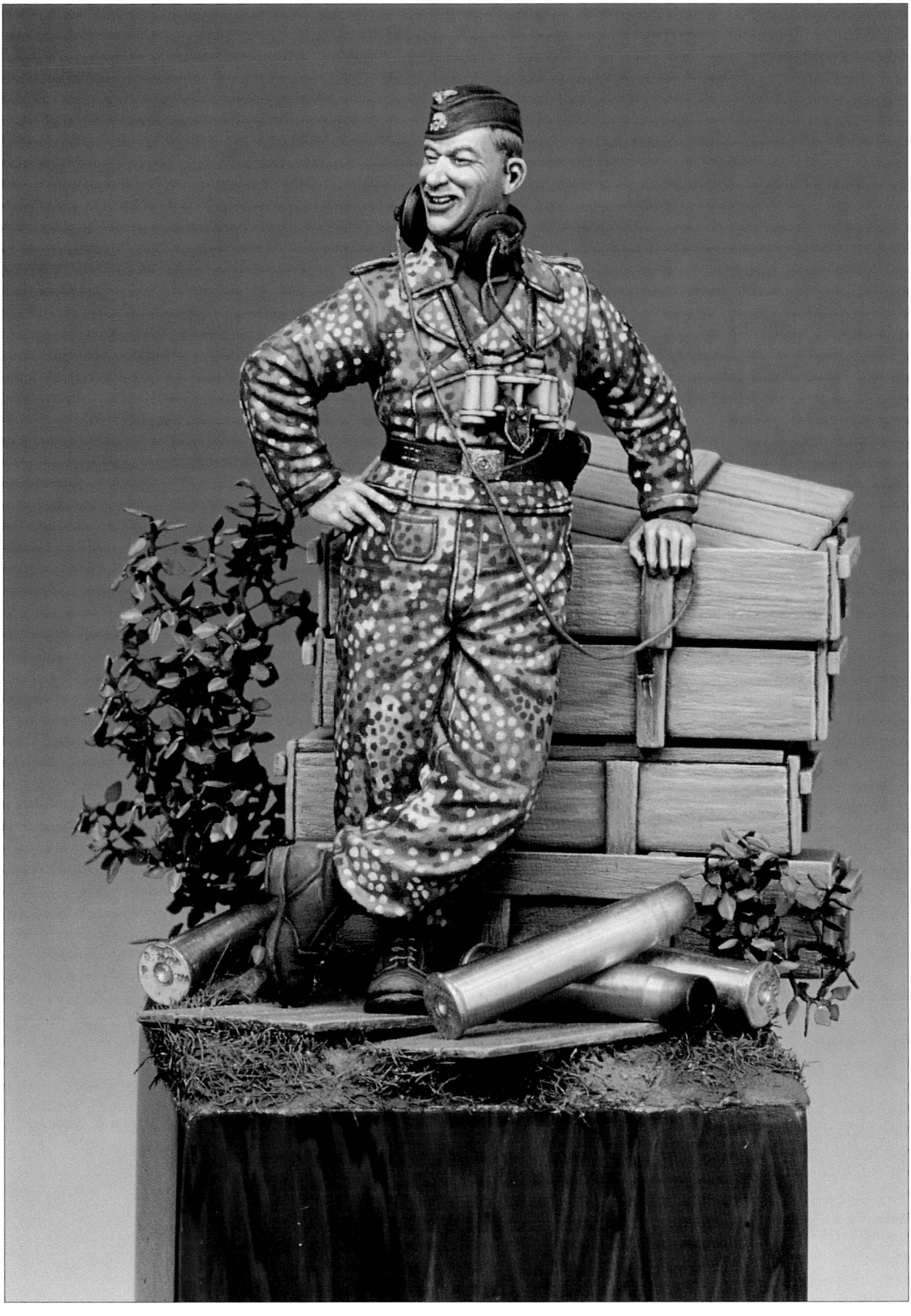

Colour chart no. 2: Dot/Pea Pattern

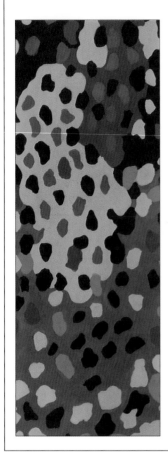

Base colour

	Mix of colours:	US Field Drab 873	English Uniform 921	German Camouflage Black Brown 822
	Mixing ratio:	5	1	1

Medium Green

	Mix of colours:	Reflective Green 890		
	Mixing ratio:	–		

Light Green

	Mix of colours:	Sunny Skin Tone 845	SS Camouflage Bright Green 833	Military Green 975
	Mixing ratio:		5	1

Dark Green

	Mix of colours:	Military Green 975	Black 950	
	Mixing ratio:	2	1	

Sand/Pink spots

	Mix of colours:	Sunny Skin Tone 845	Salmon Rose 835	English Uniform 921
	Mixing ratio:	3	4	1

Grenadiers, 12th SS-Panzer-Division 'Hitler Jügend', Normandy, 1944

Subject:	Grenadiers, 12th SS-Panzer-Division 'Hitler Jügend', Normandy, 1944
Project overview:	Re-modelling and super-detailing stock plastic figures; and painting the Oak Leaf Spring Pattern and Italian camouflage.
Modeller:	Calvin Tan
Skill level:	Advanced
Base kit:	Dragon Models 6110: SS-Grenadiers, SS-Pz.Gren.Rgt.25, HJ Division (Norrey-Enbessin 1944)
Scale:	1/35
Additional detailing sets used:	Aber PE 35A35 – German Soldier's Gear WW II
	Aber PE 35A71 – German MG34 & MG43 ammo boxes
	Tamiya 35204 – German Infantry Weapons Set A (Early/Mid WWII)
	Tamiya 35205 – German Infantry Weapons Set B (Mid/Late WWII)
	Royal Models RM 203 – German Army Equipment
	New Connection Models – MG42
	Hornet Models HH 06
	Hornet Models HH 13
	Groundwork and vegetation: Scale Link SLF039 – Leaves-Elm/Beech, Aber PE 35D01 – Ivy Leaf.
	Dry transfers: Archer Transfers SS Uniform Patches (FG35042A).
Tools and materials:	M-Tools MT 25018 Diamond File
	Gunze Sanyo GNZB 517 – Mr. Resin Primer Spray
Paints:	Vallejo Model Colour: Brass 801, German Camouflage Beige WWII 821, German Camouflage Pale Brown 825, SS Camouflage Bright Green 833, Salmon Rose 835, Sunny Skin Tone 845, Leather Brown 871, US Field Drab 873, Beige Brown 875, Reflective Green 890, Dark Prussian 899, English Uniform 921, Russian Uniform 924, Black 950, White 951, Military Green 975, Flat Brown 984, Deck Tan 986.
	Humbrol enamels: Flat Black 33, Super Silver 11.
	Gunze Sanyo lacquer-based paints: Flat Black 33, Character Yellow 109.
	Winsor & Newton oil paints: Prussian Blue, Raw Umber.

Introduction

The beginning of World War II witnessed a revolutionary display of Blitzkrieg tactics by the German Army, which changed the face of modern mechanised warfare. The combined arms of the Luftwaffe and Wehrmacht worked in tandem, yielding spectacular results. On the field of battle, armour and infantry forces worked closely together, forming the nucleus of each mechanised combat team; this explains why most model displays of World War II German armour would seem incomplete if not for the incorporation of a few infantry figures to depict that relationship.

Although the figure market was once dominated by both resin and white-metal figure manufacturers, plastic kit manufacturers like Tamiya, Dragon Models and Tristar have responded by bringing us many a quality release of infantry figure sets. Despite the lack of finesse, injection-moulded figures have proven to be a big hit amongst AFV, diorama and figure modellers for their inexpensive prices compared to resin and metal figures. Furthermore, their figure parts are broken down at the generic joints, allowing for endless conversion possibilities with other kits.

Exploiting the attributes of plastic moulded figure kits, this depiction of two Grenadiers from the 12th SS-Panzer-Division 'Hitler Jügend' demonstrates the process of remodelling, superdetailing and presentation of a historical subject in its natural setting.

Converting the figures

 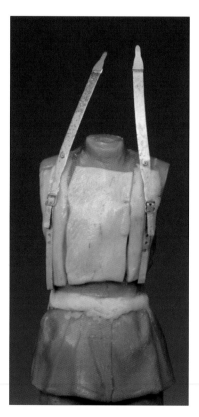 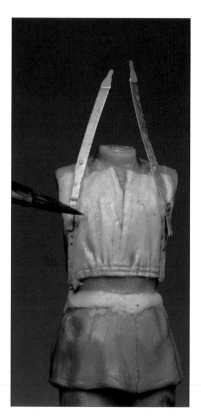

1. The NCO (SS-Scharführer) and MG42 gunner/Private (MG-Schütze) were lengthened at the waist with epoxy putty to match the anatomical proportion of the replacement heads from Hornet Models HH06 and HH13 respectively. The young gunner was deliberately made taller to portray a more virile character as a foil to the older NCO; adding contrast and interest to an otherwise plain composition.

2. Remodelling for the SS-Scharführer began by filing away the details of the original figure with a diamond file. Sheets of thinly rolled putty were then picked up with a brush moistened with Gunze Sanyo Thinner and applied onto the sanded surface. Photo-etch webbing from Aber PE 35A35 German Soldier's Gear WW II was carefully placed and positioned onto the soft putty.

3. The collar vents and elastic waist lining of the smock were fashioned using a No. 15 Swann Morton scalpel. Creases radiating from the elastic waist band were modelled with a thinner-moistened 000 brush.

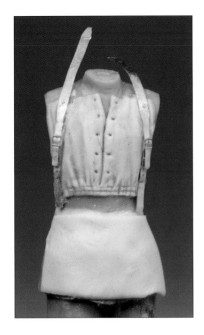

5. The MP40 magazine pouches came from Tamiya 35204 German Infantry Weapons Set A (Early/Mid WWII) and separated into their respective segments.

4. The eyelets for the collar vents were made with a sewing needle and left to cure, before another sheet of rolled putty was applied below to form the skirting of the smock.

6. They were reattached to a thin piece of newspaper, which formed the new backing of the magazine pouch.

7. The magazine pouches were attached to the soft putty on the smock skirting, and the creases radiating from both the elastic waistband and belt were modelled with a thinner-moistened 000 brush. Note how the magazine pouch curves to adhere to the contours of the smock. A thin sausage of putty was extended from the collar vents wrapped around the neck to form the collar of the smock.

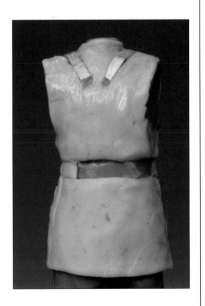

8. The soft putty was feathered into the rest of the smock, and the binoculars from Tamiya 35204 German Infantry Weapons Set A (Early/Mid WWII) were set into the chest of the figure.

9. Details on the back of the original figure were scraped off with a scalpel blade and later smoothed with a diamond file.

10. The loose ends of the webbing yoke were attached onto the figure with superglue before sheets of thinly rolled putty were applied.

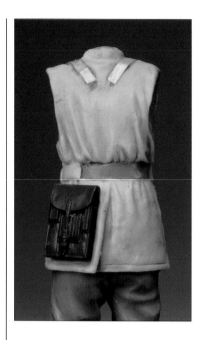
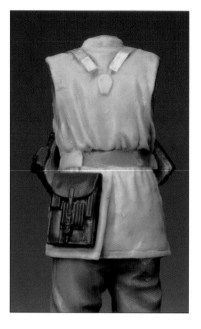
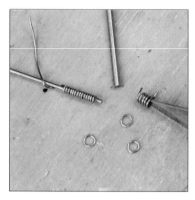

11. The leather map case from Tamiya 35204 German Infantry Weapons Set A (Early/Mid WWII) was impressed into the soft putty and the creases modelled with a thinner-moistened brush.

12. When dry, the leather tab for the 'O' ring for the back strap was made from a thin sheet of putty fashioned with a brush.

13. The 'O' rings were made by wrapping thin copper wire around the end of the drill bit and slicing with a blade.

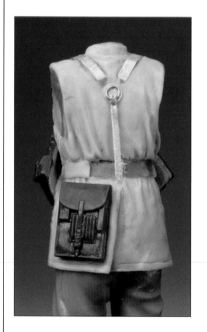

14. The 'O' ring was attached together with the back strap onto the leather tab before the putty set.

15. The loose end of the back strap was held down with a strip of rolled putty and its excess trimmed off with a scalpel. The securing loops of the 'O' rings were also made from a thinner strip of rolled putty. The map case was removed from the smock so as to facilitate the modelling of the bread bag from putty.

16. A strip of rolled putty was applied around the foundation mass of the bread bag to create the edge of the cover flap. The seams were blended in with a jeweller's metal burnisher.

17. The canteen from Tamiya 35204 German Infantry Weapons Set A (Early/Mid WWII) was impressed into the setting putty for a natural fit. The connecting loops of the 'Y' frame yoke were modelled with triangular strips of rolled putty.

18. The belt and bread bag were sanded to size with a diamond file and 400-grit sandpaper respectively.

19. Details on the bread bag were modelled from rolled putty and added with a thinner-moistened brush. The steel helmet was a spare one, which I modified from Tamiya 35204 German Infantry Weapons Set A (Early/Mid WWII).

21. ABOVE The map case was secured onto a vice clamp and the sides furrowed with a triangular diamond file.

20. Relief on the elastic waist lining was enhanced with a thin, narrow strip of putty applied over it and modelled with a fine-tipped brush. Note the binocular strap also modelled from rolled putty.

22. LEFT The accordion-expanding side flap was next modelled from a thin strip of rolled putty with a 000 pointed brush.

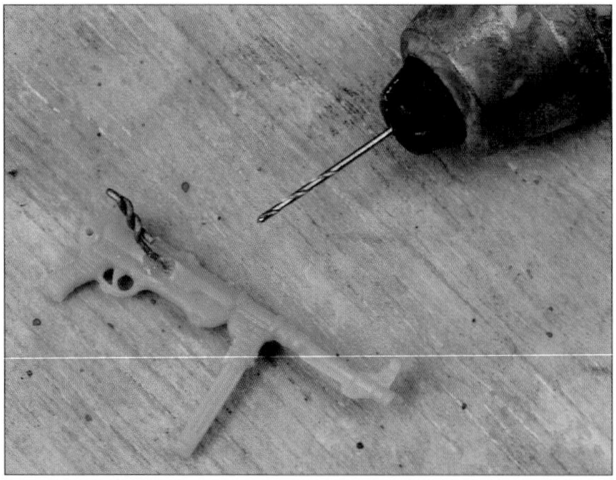

23. Two holes were drilled (one at the swivel of the folding stock and another at the carrying handle to accommodate a braided wire to form the arm for the gripping hand) onto the MP40 with a 0.5mm drill bit from M-Tools MT 25044.

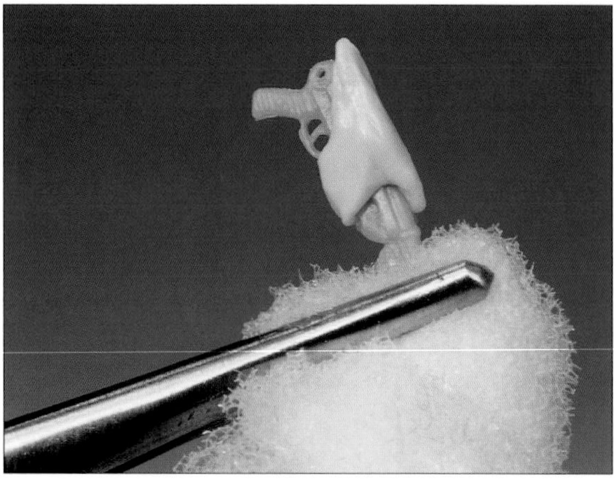

24. The arm was coated with putty and a basic mass of the hand was formed with a knife and brush. The plastic barrel was wrapped with sponge to prevent breakage and warping when the putty is baked in the oven.

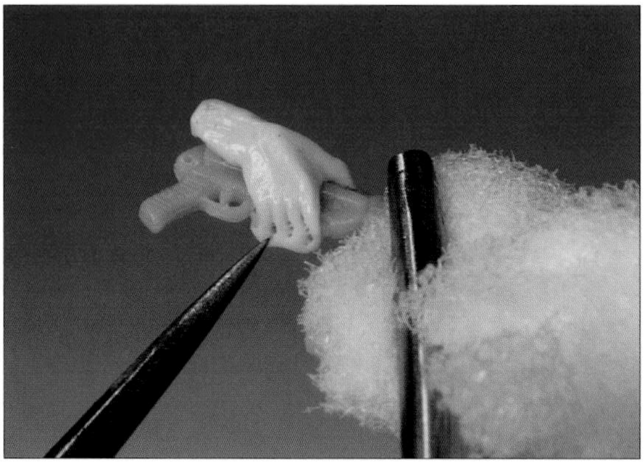

25. The digits were divided with a knife and shaped with a needle.

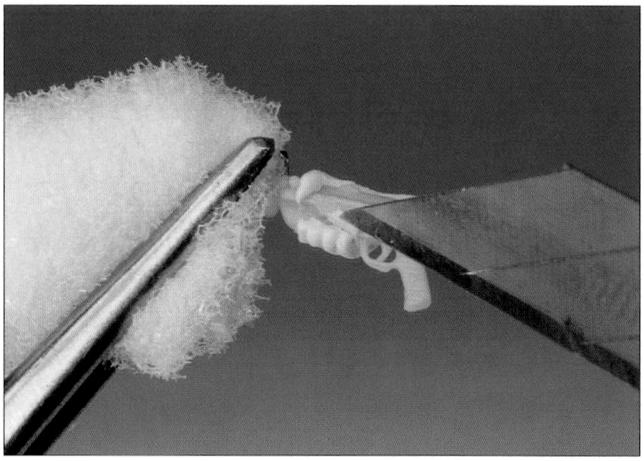

26. Excess amounts were trimmed off with a sharp blade, and it was left to cure.

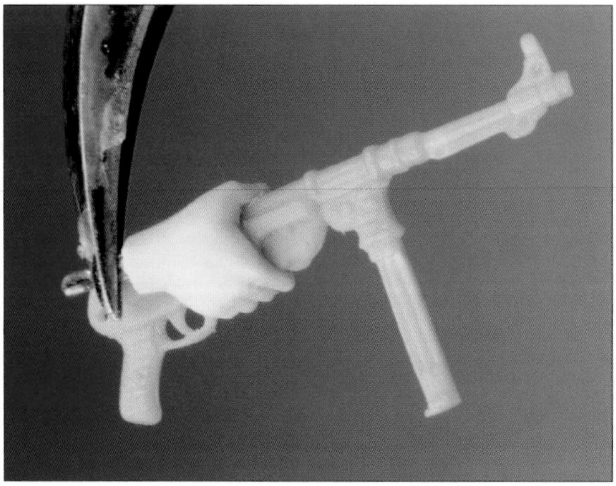

27. The hand was further refined with some light carving to better define the shapes and details.

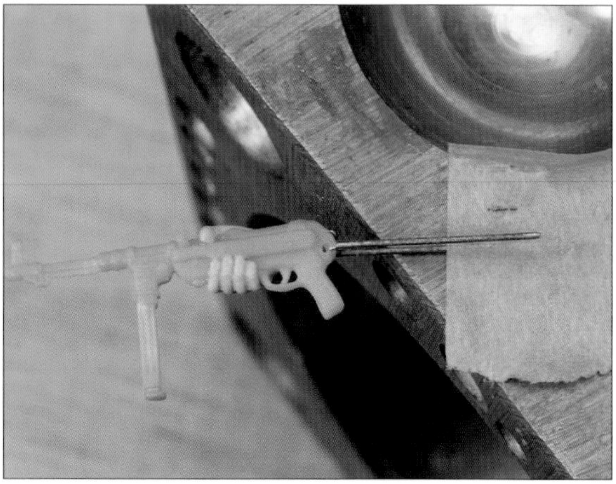

28. A fuse wire was inserted and bent through the hole at the back of the MP40.

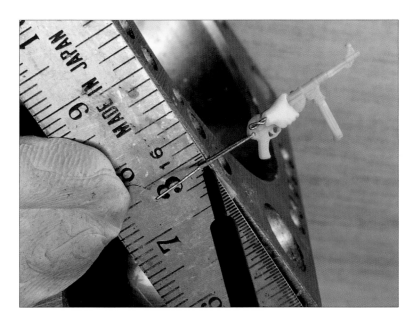

29. While one side was laid flat with a metal ruler, a round punch was hammered at the end to flatten the wire to form the swivel bracket for the shoulder rest.

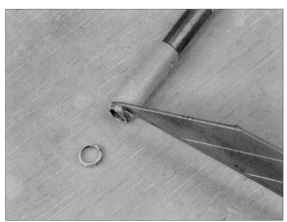

30. A ring was sliced from a brass tube with a sharp blade, using a thick coil of masking tape to maintain the horizontal alignment.

31. It was attached to a piece of double-sided tape affixed to a block of wood and filed to size with a diamond file.

32. It was then clamped together using a pair of pliers, and squashed into an oval shape.

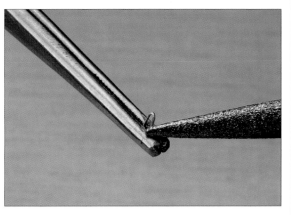

33. A final brush with the diamond file shaped the form of the shoulder rest before it was attached to the swivel bracket.

34. The collars of the tunic were next modelled in. The right hand gripping the MP40 was attached to the arm, which was made from braided fuse wire coated with epoxy putty.

35. This was left to cure before a thin sheet of rolled putty was applied over.

36. The draping folds were modelled with a brush and needle.

37. Thin strips of epoxy putty were applied to create the overlapping folds.

38. They were blended with a brush and jeweller's burnisher.

39. The raised left arm was modelled using the same method as for the right one.

40. The bulk of the form and the tight compression of the folds were built up using strips of rolled putty.

41. A brush moistened with thinners was passed over the seams of the strips to smooth and 'melt' them.

42. A thin sheet of putty was applied over the helmet to create the camouflage helmet cover.

43. It was shaped with a 0 brush.

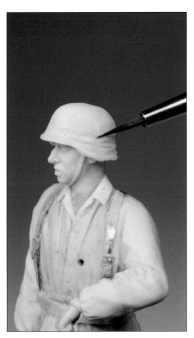

44. The seams were created with a scalpel, and the creases modelled in with a 000 brush.

45. The creases and folds of the trousers were relatively well modelled on the original figure but lacked the desired bulk. This was rectified by applying thin sheets of rolled putty over them, and blending in with a brush.

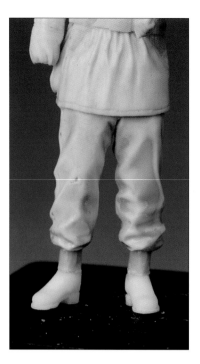

46. The correction completed.

47. The original leggings were removed with a scalpel, and new shoes were added from my spares box. The details were subsequently added using thin sheets of rolled putty.

48. Foliage loops and drawstrings were made from thin strips of putty and attached with a moistened brush.

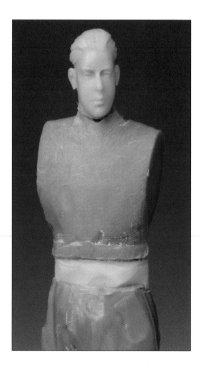

49. A front view of the remodelled figure.

50. A rear view of the remodelled figure.

51. Details on the torso of the MG42 gunner were removed with a scalpel and shaped with a diamond file.

52. Modelling of the creases and webbing on the overalls followed the same pattern as for the NCO figure. The P08 Luger holster and MG42 gunner's belt pouch came from 35205 German Infantry Weapons Set B (Mid/Late WWII).

53. The opening flap for the overalls was modelled from a strip of thinly rolled putty.

54. The sides were merged with a jeweller's burnisher and a moist brush, and the seams impressed with a blade. The gas mask canister carrying strap and the sides of the gunner's belt pouch were modelled from strips of rolled putty.

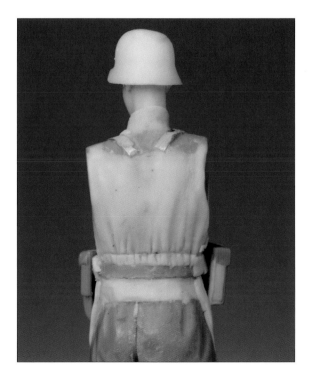

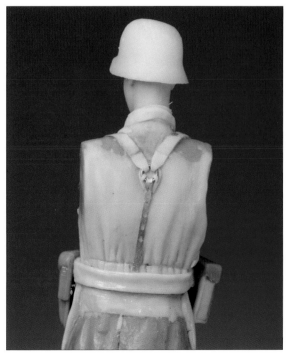

55. The elastic waist for the overalls was modelled in the same fashion as the NCO's smock.

56. More details were added to the back of the figure with rolled putty.

57. ABOVE The resting hand on the MG42 was modelled from putty and shaped with a blade when dry.

58. RIGHT The arms and sleeves were modelled with a needle impressed into the soft putty in the tight areas of the folds.

59. The belt of resin MG42 rounds was from New Connections Models, and it was attached to the centre of the collars with a tiny drop of superglue.

60. Heat emitted from a burning incense stick was used to soften the belt and contour it around the collar before it was secured with a drop of superglue applied carefully with a sharp blade.

61. The chest pockets were modelled with rolled putty shaped with a sharp blade and moist brush.

62. The pockets took shape, and the collars were applied around the neck of the figure.

63. Buttons were modelled from square bits of putty and shaped with a moist brush and needle.

64. The links for the MG42 belts were finally added with finely sliced bits of rolled putty applied with a moist brush. A final light wash of clear varnish over the setting putty helped seal the putty to the resin surface.

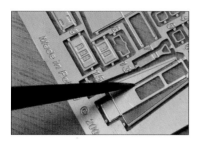

65. The MG42 ammunition box was from Aber PE 35A71 German MG34 & MG43 Ammo Boxes. Lines were scored with a sharp needle along the furrows to enable a sharp bend at the edge of the lid and container.

66. A thick paste of Gunze Sanyo Surfacer 500 was applied to the corners of the depressions on the lids and sides of the ammunition box to create an impressed, stamped appearance.

67. Tiny parts, like the hinges and swivels, were formed on the fret for easy handling (especially important if you have clumsy hands, like me!) Here, a section of a hinge has been formed against the side of a drill bit.

68. Once removed from the fret, small parts were attached to a strip of masking tape, for easy handling and faster recovery when dropped.

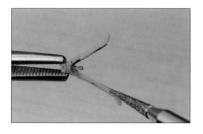

69. The bipod for the MG42 was a stock component, with the insides furrowed with a conical diamond blur.

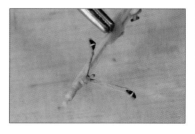

70. The completed bipod with the spiked legs made from paper.

71. The completed figure of the MG42 gunner.

72. Another view of the completed MG42 gunner. Note the carrying straps for the gas mask canister made from paper.

73. The completed pair was placed on the groundwork, built up from compressed foam; the stone ridge was sculpted from epoxy putty.

74. The groundwork was made by incorporating the techniques described in the previous builds; it was undercoated with black and painted using washes and light dry-brushing.

75. The completed groundwork. The fallen foliage comprised photo-etched parts from Scale Link SLF039 Leaves-Elm/Beech and Aber PE 35D01 Ivy Leafs, and was painted with various shades of English Uniform, Red Leather, Military Green and Yellow Ochre.

Painting the figures

76. The NCO's smock (in the Oak-Leaf camouflage pattern) was undercoated with a 3:1 mix of German Camouflage Pale Brown 825 and Flat Brown 984.

77. The clumps of light green (mixed from 2:5:1:2 Sunny Skin Tone 845, SS Camouflage Bright Green 833, Military Green 975, and English Uniform 921) were loosely outlined with dark green (consisting of a 2:1 mix of Medium Green 975 and Black 950).

78. The pattern was further refined with the medium green A (4:1 mix of Reflective Green 890 and Flat Brown 984) and medium green B (Military Green 975).

79. Details of the uniform and webbing were shaded and highlighted. The MP40 pouches were painted with Russian Uniform 924, highlighted with Sunny Skin Tone 845, and shaded with Sepia ink. The scarf was painted with a light blue to break up the monotony of drab colours.

80. The map case and bread bag were painted and detailed.

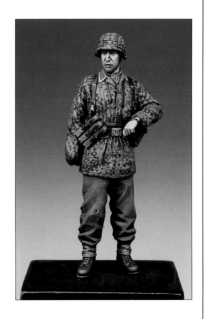

81. The painting of the figure concluded with the same techniques and colours described in the first chapter featuring the SS-Sturmmann, 1st SS-Panzer-Division.

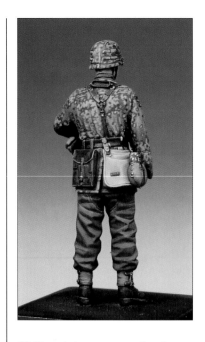

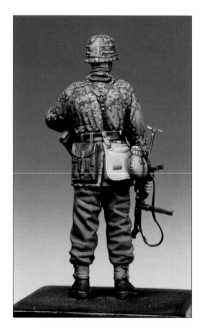

82. The painting process continued.

83. The completed figure of the SS-Scharführer. Note the MP40 sling and buckle made from paper stiffened with superglue.

84. The completed SS-Scharführer.

85. The overalls worn by the MG-Schütze were undercoated with a 1:3:3 mix of Reflective Green 890, German Field Grey WWII 830 and German Camouflage Extra Dark Green 896.

86. The sand yellow patches consisted of a 3:2:1 mix of German Camouflage Orange Ochre 824, Tan Yellow 912, and Dark Sand 847 and was applied in successive layers. Shadows were loosely created by incorporating more English Uniform 921 into the mix.

87. The brown patches were made up of a 1:1 mix of German Camouflage Black Brown 822 and Flat Brown 984. Highlights and shadows were created by varying the quantity of Flat Brown and Black Brown.

88. The camouflage was further refined and weathered with thin glazes of German Camouflage Beige 821 and US Field Drab 873.

89. Details of the uniform were defined with Black for the dark lines and Sunny Skin Tone 845 for the edges. The bullet belt was painted with a lacquer-based Gold paint from a felt-tipped permanent marker. 801 Brass was subsequently carefully scrubbed over to enhance the brightness.

90. The individual bullets were painted with copper and highlighted with a glaze of Brass 801. The links were painted with a light glaze of silver before sealing them with a thin coat of gloss varnish.

91. The boots were painted with Flat Brown, shaded with Sepia and highlighted with Beige Brown. The MG42 ammunition box was painted with Military Green 975. Weathering was completed with glazes of US Field Drab 873 and German Camouflage Beige WWII 821 mixed in varying quantities, applied to the boots and other areas of wear.

92. The preliminary stages of painting and weathering completed.

93. The carrying handles for the MG ammunition box were made from a thinly rolled sausage of putty and attached with a thinner-moistened brush.

94. The carrying straps for the gas mask canister were made from paper stiffened with superglue, and were attached to their respective locations.

95. Likewise, the MG sling was made from paper with the attachment swivels made from fine wire and bits of putty. Collar patches came from SS Uniform Patches (FG35042A).

96. The completed figure with the helmet camouflage cover painted in the Oak-Leaf Spring pattern.

ABOVE, RIGHT, AND OPPOSITE PAGE **The completed figure.**

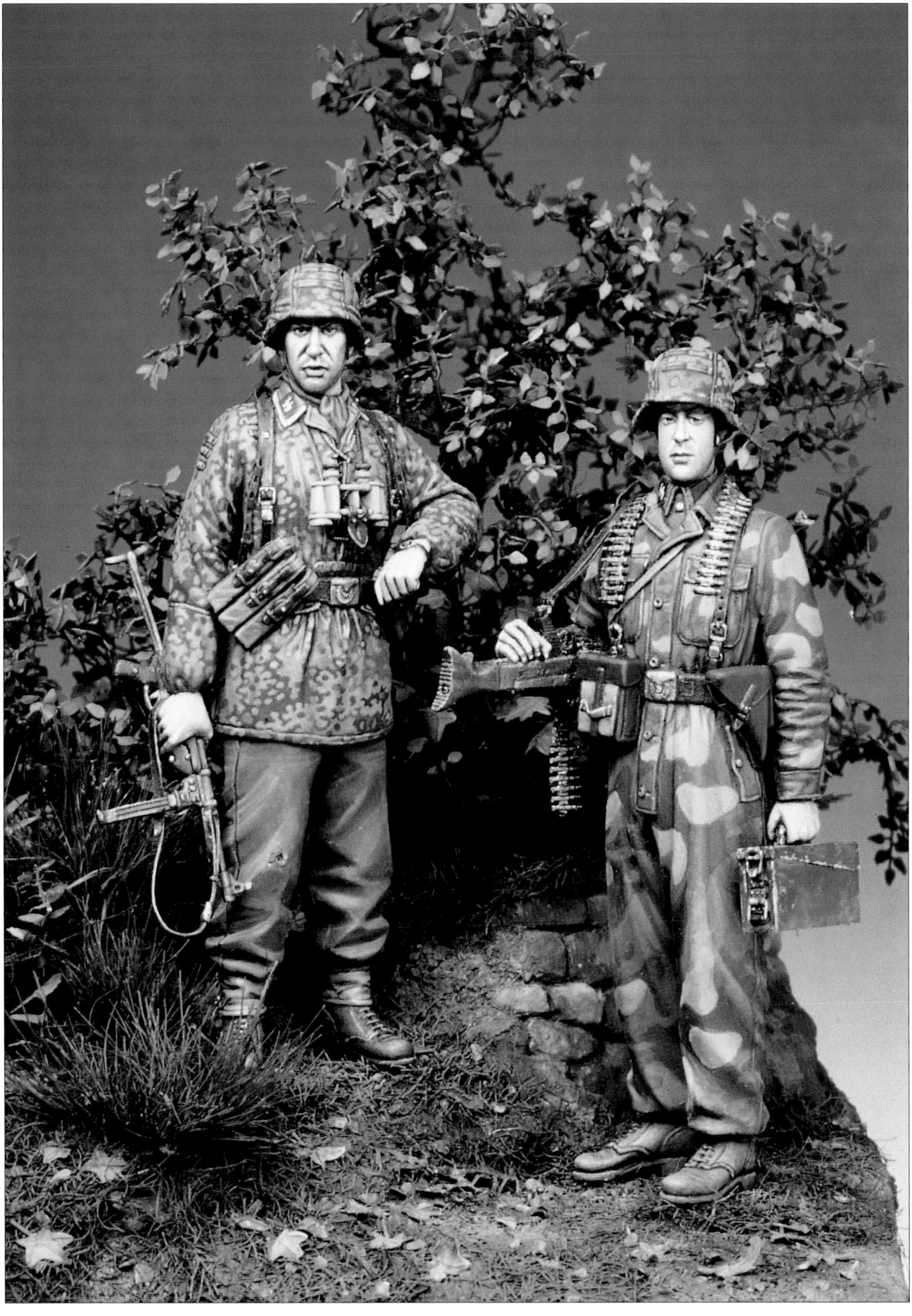

Colour chart no. 3: Italian Pattern

Base colour

	Mix of colours:	Reflective Green 890	German Field Grey WWII 830	German Camouflage Extra Dark Green 896
	Mixing ratio:	1	3	3

Brown

	Mix of colours:	German Camouflage Black Brown 822	Flat Brown 984
	Mixing ratio:	1	1

Sand Yellow

	Mix of colours:	German Camouflage Orange Ochre 824	Tan Yellow 912	Dark Sand 847
	Mixing ratio:	3	2	1

Colour chart no. 4: Oak-Leaf Pattern (Spring)

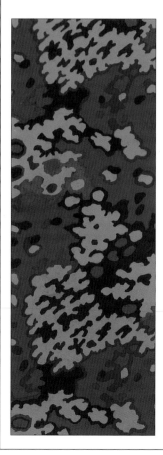

Base colour

	Mix of colours:	German Camouflage Pale Brown 825	Flat Brown 984
	Mixing ratio:	3	1

Medium Green A

	Mix of colours:	Reflective Green 890	Flat Brown 984
	Mixing ratio:	4	1

Medium Green B

	Mix of colours:	Military Green 975
	Mixing ratio:	–

Dark Green

	Mix of colours:	Military Green 975	Black 950
	Mixing ratio:	2	1

Light Green

	Mix of colours:	Sunny Skin Tone 845	SS Camouflage Bright Green 833	Military Green 975	English Uniform 921
	Mixing ratio:	2	5	1	2

'Salvation': SS-Schütze, 3rd SS-Panzer-Division 'Totenkopf', Vienna, 1945

Subject:	*'Salvation': SS-Schütze, 3rd SS-Panzer-Division 'Totenkopf', Vienna, 1945*
Project overview:	*This special build explores modelling as 'artistic expression' as opposed to purely historical representation.*
Modeller:	*Calvin Tan*
Skill level:	*Master*
Base kits:	*MIG Productions Destroyed T34 Hull (RW.35-018). Hornet Models (HH12). Dry transfers: Archer Transfers SS Uniform Patches (FG35042A), Heer Shoulder Boards for Panzer Crews (FG35043B).*
Scale:	*1/35*
Paints:	*Vallejo Model Colour: German Camouflage Beige WWII 821, German Camouflage Pale Brown 825, SS Camouflage Bright Green 833, Salmon Rose 835, Sunny Skin Tone 845, Leather Brown 871, US Field Drab 873, Beige Brown 875, Reflective Green 890, Russian Green 894, Dark Prussian 899, English Uniform 921, Russian Uniform 924, Black 950, White 951, Military Green 975, Flat Brown 984, Deck Tan 986*

Introduction

As the war on the Eastern Front drew to a close in the spring of 1945, numerous desperate battles were fought by Waffen-SS forces. One such unit was the infamous 3rd SS-Panzer-Division 'Totenkopf'; which after the ill-fated offensive at Lake Balaton in Hungary withdrew to Austria before capitulating to US Army forces on 9 May 1945. Severely understrength with no hope of re-supply and reinforcement reaching them, soldiers of the 'Totenkopf' division fought a desperate battle to avoid capture by Soviet forces. Survival became the main hope for many weary men as their defensive positions were compromised and their situation worsened; and it was perhaps valour, sacrifice and faith that prevailed amidst a time of futile struggle towards an inevitable end. This is the overall mood and feel I wanted to recreate in this artistic vignette.

Modelling works usually celebrate valour and bravado on the battlefield. However, inspired by biblical resonances, I drew upon the perhaps controversial idea of portraying a Waffen-SS soldier seeking hope and personal salvation in a time of grave danger. Numerous symbolic aspects have been employed to convey a much deeper message. The soldier is a helpless pawn embroiled in a dramatic struggle of life and death. The choice of 1/35 scale reinforces the image of the fragility of human life. The wrecked T-34 chassis, which serves to elevate the height of the kneeling figure, is juxtaposed with the red bricks and black ashes to signify human sacrifice and material destruction.

Sculpting the figure

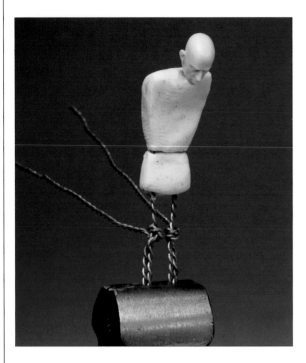

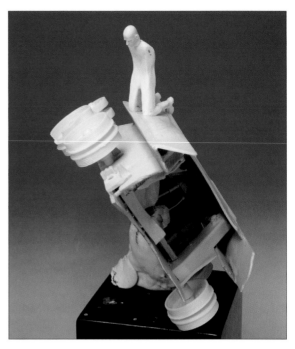

1. Incorporating a spare head from Hornet Models HH12, the pose was rigged up with an armature made from braided wire and epoxy putty.

2. The bulk of the posture was built up with epoxy putty and left to set on the T-34 wreckage so as to allow a good 'sit'.

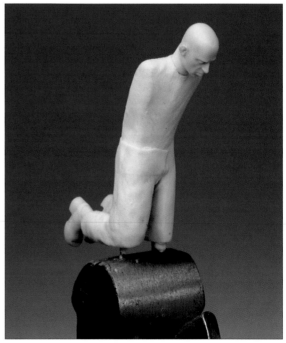

3. The armature was filed to shape with a diamond file. The boots were resin castings from my spares box.

4. The winter trousers were made from thinly rolled out sheets of epoxy putty placed over the armature. Note that only one side was made so as to give ample time to model a small surface area.

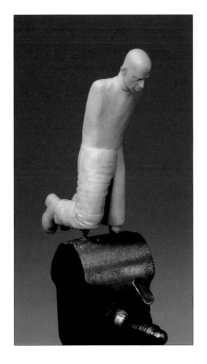

5. The creases were first modelled in with a brush moistened with Gunze Sanyo Thinner and with a sharp needle after the putty had firmed up for about an hour.

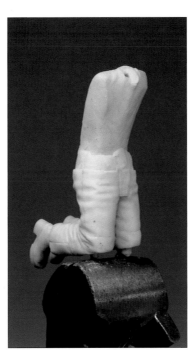

6. The first trouser sleeve was left to set before the second sleeve and fly flap were modelled.

7. The form of the M43 tunic was created with sheets of thinly rolled putty attached and shaped with a moist brush.

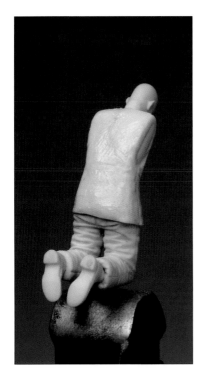

8. The back of the figure showing the bare form of the tunic.

9. Creases and details were sculpted and refined.

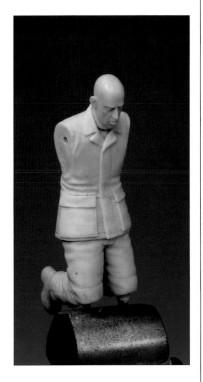

10. Superficial details and features, such as the waist pockets and collars, were modelled in.

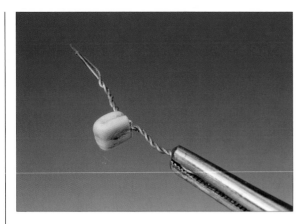

11. The cupped hands took shape by attaching two square slabs of putty to a piece of braided fuse wire.

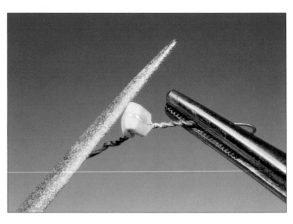

12. They were left to set and filed to shape with a diamond file.

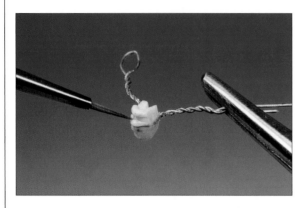

13. The fingers were added on individually with the aid of a thinner-moistened brush.

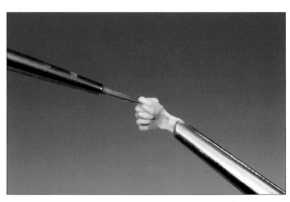

14. The shapes of the fingers were refined with a 000 pointed brush.

15. The final details, such as the knuckles, were carved out with a scalpel blade.

16. The armature for the arm was rigged up with braided wire and epoxy putty, and was propped up with Blue-Tac while the putty accommodating the cupped hand cured.

17. The joints for the arms were frozen with putty. The sleeve openings for both arms also took shape after some light carving.

18. The hair and creases on the arms were modelled next.

19. The buttons on the tunic were created by attaching small squares of rolled-out putty with a 000 thinner-moistened brush, and bevelling the corners to create a circular disc.

20. The completed figure with the hands primed with Gunze Sanyo Surfacer 500.

21. Another view of the completed figure.

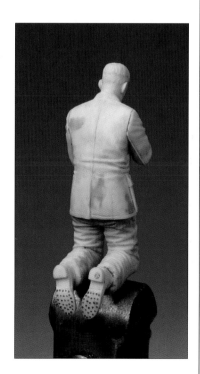

22. The hobnails on the marching boots were made from sliced bits of stretched sprue attached with Tamiya Extra Thin Cement.

Creating the base

23. The built-up T-34 wreckage from MIG Productions primed with Gunze Resin Primer.

24. The wreckage was undercoated in black, and was propped up and secured into the base with epoxy putty.

25. To form the bricks, a jig was created from the edge of a scrap piece of wood to equally dice strips of compressed foam.

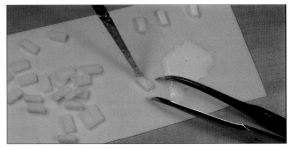

26. The foam was textured with plaster, painted over, and left to dry on the smooth surface of sheet styrene.

27. Once dry, the plaster coated foam was prized off the styrene and attached with a solution of white glue and plaster.

28. The debris was formed by breaking off the perfectly formed sections of bricks and texturing them with Gunze Sanyo Surfacer 500.

29. Cross beams made from sheet styrene and spare materials from random sources were embedded into the epoxy putty groundwork. A final sprinkle of fine gravel from a nearby construction yard completed the groundwork before it was secured with a light mist of hair spray.

30. The whole set up was airbrushed with Gunze Sanyo Flat Black to establish the shadows.

31. Features such as the wreckage, beams and brick sections were loosely painted with their respective mid tones to establish colour composition. The idea here was just to play around with the colours, with the final presentation in mind.

32. To attain a more natural and spontaneous diffusion of shades and tones on a wrecked surface, I borrowed a technique from watercolour painting. A mix consisting of 1:2:3 of Tamiya Flat Base X21, Vallejo Flat Brown 984, and Orange Brown 981 was heavily diluted with 5 parts of water and generously applied over the surface.

33. A second batch of wash of the same consistency with a 1:2 mix of Flat Base and Black 950 was applied almost immediately and allowed to 'mingle' with the rust colour.

34. Sepia ink was randomly dripped and allowed to diffuse with the rest of the colours to create a melange of tones and shades.

35. When dry, the effects were substantially subdued due to the high percentage of Flat Base incorporated into the mixes. Adding more Flat Base would also produce an ash-like effect that's quite random; do capitalise on the water marks to create natural burnt stains on the surface.

Painting and finishing

36. With the face rendered, the base colours for the tunic (1:1 mix of Extra Dark Green and Field Grey), winter trousers in Oak Leaf pattern autumn scheme (7:1:1 mix of German Camouflage Beige 821, English Uniform 921, and German Camo Black Brown Brown 822) and hair (English Uniform 921) were loosely glazed onto the figure for a quick colour sketch.

37. The top of the hull was joined to the rest of the groundwork and painted with varying shades of Military Green 975, Russian Green 894, Black 950, SS Bright Cam Bright Green 833, and US Field Drab 873. The figure was transferred onto the groundwork to better visualise the final composition of colours.

38. The figure was returned to the painting stand and the dark brown patches were painted in with German Camo Black Brown Brown 822.

39. The yellow 'large land masses' consisting of a 6:1 mix of German Camouflage Orange Ochre 824 and Orange Brown 981 were painted on in thin successive layers to prevent an unnecessary build up of paint. The shadows were created by incorporating more Orange Brown 981 and German Camo Black Brown 822 into the base colour.

40. The opacity of the yellow patches was built up with successive thin glazes of paint. The yellow 'large land masses' were outlined with two shades of medium brown colours – (A) a 1:3:2 mix of Cam Black Brown 822, Flat Brown 984, Orange Brown 981; and (B) a 3:1 mix of Cam Pale Brown 825 and Cam Black Brown 822.

41. The strong shadows were subdued with repeated washes of Extra Dark Green over the affected spots. Be careful not to unload too much paint from the brush as it will increase the appearance of water marks on the paint surface.

42. The highlights were applied with successive washes of Extra Dark Green 896, German Field Grey WW2 830, and German Camouflage Beige 821.

43. The seams of the tunic and trousers were outlined with a Sepia ink and Black paint mix. Highlights along the edges were applied with glazes of German Camouflage Beige 821 and US Field Drab 873.

44. The collar tabs from Archer Transfers were applied and details such as the buttons and scarf were painted.

45. The right arm was attached to the rest of the figure and cavities were patched with putty. The 'horseshoe' plates on the heels were made from thin strips of epoxy putty.

46. The figure received shoulder boards and arm bands from Archer Transfers.

47. The figure was then shaded with washes of Black 950 and Sepia ink.

48. The hair was highlighted with glazes of English Uniform, Deep Yellow 915, and Pale Sand 837. Shadows were painted with Russian Uniform WW2 924 and US Olive Drab 889.

49. The figure was attached to the wreckage. The paint chips were painted with varying mixes of Black 950 and Red Leather 818. A highlight colour consisting of Military Green 975 mixed with varying quantities of German Camouflage Beige 821 and US Field Drab 873 was applied along the bottom of the chips to enhance the impression of relief on a battered surface.

50. A final glaze consisting of various mixes of German Camo Black Brown 822, German Field Grey WW2 830, German Camouflage Beige 821, and US Field Drab 873 were randomly glazed onto the highlights of the figure, again to add tonal variations to the tunic.

ABOVE AND RIGHT **The completed figure 'in prayer'.**

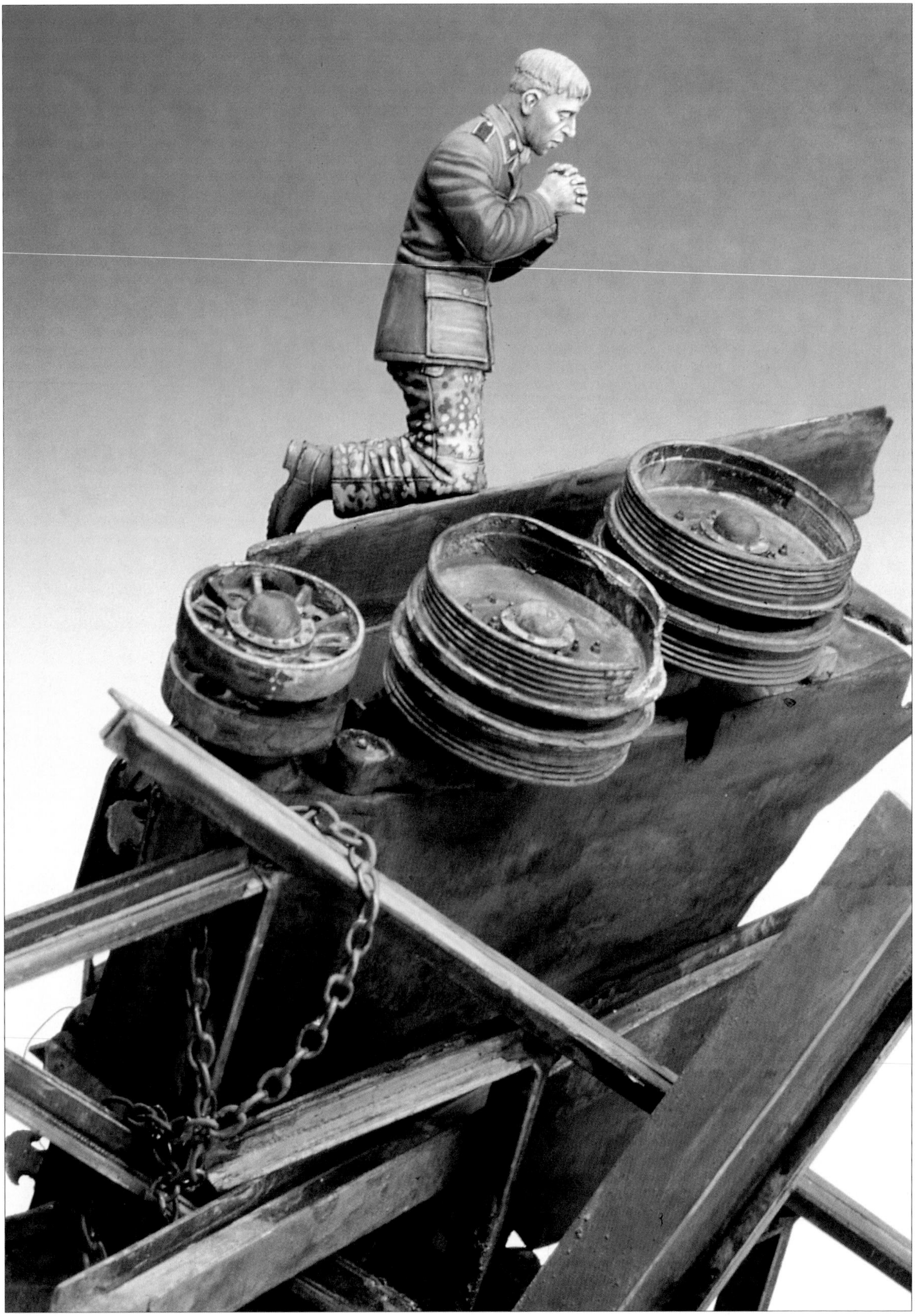

Endnote

Historical miniature modellers often strive for authenticity of historical subject representation and finesse in visual presentation. One cannot deny the value of authentic historical research, which has provided many a vivid setting for us modellers. But regardless of how accurately or beautifully rendered a vignette might be, the one element needed to make a figure-centred work come to life is the presence of humanity in the works. Studying the work of master modellers like Shep Paine and Bill Horan will reveal that the universal depiction of the human spirit fills the void, creating enduring masterpieces of art. Perceiving a miniature soldier as a human being rather than just a subject for historical representation will steer you towards a more convincing depiction of such subjects. Characterisation of the figure will further engage the viewer, helping to add reality to mere superficial ornamentation and 'breathing life' into the figure.

To ensure the communicative power of this build, the story had to be at the centre of the piece before all other considerations. There are situations where one must take artistic liberties in order to deliver certain messages and express certain concepts. Sculpting and rendering techniques should be adapted by the modeller to suit the demands of the build. I stress the word 'adapt' because there is a tendency (of which I myself am guilty) to focus too much on the rendering process, thus deviating from the focus of communication for the sake of unnecessary ornamentation. Such are the pit-falls that sometimes deny a very well rendered creation the expressive edge it truly deserves. A fine line has to be drawn at times between the focus of artistic objectivity and fun. I'm personally all for the idea of making the process of modelling fun; but somehow or other, I feel that there could still be another greater level of artistic achievement that we can attain from this constantly evolving art form, making it more than just a leisure pastime.

Colour chart no. 5: Oak-Leaf Pattern (Autumn)

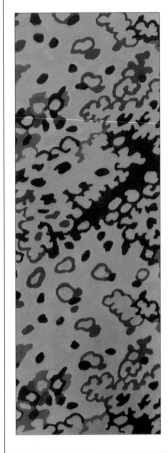

Base colour

Mix of colours:	German Camouflage Beige 821	English Uniform 921	German Camouflage Black Brown 822
Mixing ratio:	6	1	1

Medium Brown A

Mix of colours:	German Camouflage Black Brown 822	Flat Brown 984	Orange Brown 981
Mixing ratio:	1	3	2

Medium Brown B

Mix of colours:	German Camouflage Pale Brown 825	German Camouflage Black Brown 822
Mixing ratio:	3	1

Dark Brown

Mix of colours:	German Camouflage Black Brown 822
Mixing ratio:	–

Ochre Yellow

Mix of colours:	German Camouflage Orange Ochre 824	Orange Brown 981
Mixing ratio:	6	1

Kits and accessories available

Recommended 1/35 plastic injection-moulded figures	
Dragon Models (DML)	6028 Tiger Aces (Normandy 1944)
	6046 8th SS Cavalry Division 'Florian Geyer'
	6059 Waffen SS Panzer Grenadiers (Kharkov 1943)
	6067 13th SS Mountain Troops 'Handschar'
	6088 Kampfgruppe Peiper (Ardennes 1944)
	6091 Ambush At Poteau (Ardennes 1944)
	6095 SS 'Totenkopf' Division (Budapest 1945)
	6110 SS-Grenadiers, SS-Pz.Gren.Rgt.25, HJ Division (Norrey-Enbessin 1944)
	6116 Panzermeyer, LSSAH Division (Mariupol 1941)
	6131 Amored Reconnaissance, SS Wiking Division
	6144 Commanders Conference (Kharkov 1943)
	6145 SS-Fallschirmjager Batallion 500 (Drvar, 1944)
	6146 SS-Sturmpionier (Eastern Front 1942)
	6161 Panzergenadiers (Arnhem 1944)
	6194 Panzergrenadiers Wiking Division (Hungary 1945)
	6159 Panzergrenadiers LAH Div. 1943 Kursk
	6162 Winter's Onset Near Moscow 1941
	6214 Panzer Crew LAH Panzer Div. Russia 1943
Tamiya Models	35196 German Front-Line Infantrymen
	35201 German Tank Crew at Rest Figure Set
	35253 German Tank Unit Front Observation Team
Tristar Model Ltd.	TS35001 German Panzer Crew (Waffen-SS in Normandy 1944)
Fine Moulds	FNMFM-09 German Tank Crew Set

Recommended 1/35 resin figures	
Gunze Sanyo	2201 Assault Gun Crew Set for Sturmgeschutz 40 Ausf G
	2202 German Infantry Set for Sturmgeschutz 40 Ausf G
	2203 Sd.Kfz. 250/1 Neu Figure Set
	2204 SS Tank Crew Letter from Home 1
	2205 SS Tank Crew Letter from Home 2
Show Modelling	SHM077F German Tank Crew Figure - Relaxed pose
Royal Models	RM-156 Waffen SS Tanker Sitting on Turret
	RM-157 Waffen SS Tanker looking thru Binoculars
	RM-163 SS Untersturmfuhrer - Staumont '44
	RM-196 Waffen SS (Ardennes) - WW II
	RM-209 SS-Panzergranadier 12th SS Normandy '44
	RM-210 SS-Panzergrenadier - Rgt. (Stoumont)
	RM-214 German Tanker
	RM-232 Waffen SS Tank Crew - 4 Partial Figures
	RM-287 SS Grenadier At Rest (1944)
	RM-294 Sleeping SS Grenadier
MA Mori	MAM-MG001 German SS NCO, Seated
	MAM-MG003 German SS Tankers
	MAM-MG004 German SS Tanker, Seated
	MAM-MG005 Schwimmwagen Driver
	MAM-MG016 SS Tanker, 1944
	MAM-MG017 SS Major, w/ Motorcycle Coat
	MAM-MG018 SS Staff Officer
	MAM-MG019 SS Corporal
	MAM-MG020 SS Tank Crew w/ Camo Overalls
	MAM-MG021 SS Tank Crew w/ Camo Overalls #2

Pegaso Models	PM-200003 - SS Standartenfuhrer, 1944
	PM-54188 - Reichsmarshall, 1944
	PM-PT012 - SS Obersturmfuhrer, 1942-1943
Soldati	SLDT-35008 - Unterscharfuhrer, Italy 1943
	SLDT-35017 - SS Scharfuhrer, 1944
	SLDT-35020 - Waffen SS, Russia 1944
	SLDT-35022 - HitlerJugend
Yosci	Y-G02 - SS Infantryman, Ardennes 1944
	Y-G05 - Kurt 'Panzer' Meyer, Kharkov 1943
	Y-G06 - German Grenadier, Kharkov 1943
	Y-G09 - Jochen Peiper, Kharkov 1943
	Y-G10 - German Officer, Berlin 1945
	Y-G13 - Kurt 'Panzer' Meyer, 1944
	Y-GSP - Michael Wittmann & Crew
TANK	TNK-35003 - German Tankers, 1944-1945
	TNK-35005 - SS Tankers #1, 1940-1945
	TNK-35006 - SS Tankers, 1943-1945
	TNK-35007 - SS Tankers, 1944-1945
	TNK-35008 - SS Tankers #2, 1940-1945
	TNK-35029 - SS Infantry #1, 1943
	TNK-35030 - SS Infantryman #1, 1943
	TNK-35031 - SS Infantry #2, 1943
	TNK-35032 - SS Infantryman #2, 1943
	TNK-35033 - SS Infantry #3, 1943
	TNK-35034 - SS Infantry #4, 1943
	TNK-35035 - SS Infantry #5, 1943
	TNK-35036 - SS Infantry #6, 1943
	TNK-35039 - SS Officer, Italy 1944
Wolf Miniatures	WM-2401 - Wounded SS Soldier
	WM-AW06 - German in Zeltbahn
	WM-AW07 - SS Grenadier
	WM-AW08 - German Machinegunner
	WM-AW09 - German Tanker
	WM-AW13 - Seated German
	WM-AW15 - German Machinegunner
	WM-AW21 - SS, Pulling on Boot
	WM-AW22 - SS Grenadier, 1944
	WM-AW26 - Barechested German
	WM-AW27 - German, Lounging
	WM-AW28 - SS Grenadier
	WM-AW29 - SS Officer

Recommended 1/35 metal/pewter figures

Takahashi Modelling	TK-01 - LSSAH NCO, Barbarossa 1941
	TK-02 - LSSAH Sergeant, Villers-Bocage 1944
	TK-8 - "LAH" SS Pz Div. Gunner & Loader
	TK-13 - German 'LAH' SS 101st Heavy Tank Battalion N.C.O.
	TK-14 - German 'LAH' SS 101st Heavy Tank Battalion Sergeant-Major
	TK-17 - German LAH SS Brig STG Commander 1941
	TK-18 - German LAH SS Brig STG Tank Crew Balkans 1941
	TK-20 - German 101st SS Heavy Tank Battalion Captain
	TK-21 - German 101st SS Heavy Tank Battalion Tank Crew
Hornet Models	HM-GH01 - SS in Camo, Walking
	HM-GH02 - SS in Camo, Walking
	HM-GH03 - SS Officer, Walking
	HM-GH05 - SS Officer in Jerkin
	HM-GH09 - German in Smock
	HM-GH12 - AFV Crewman
	HM-GH13 - AFV Crewman
	HM-GH19 - Panzer Grenadier
	HM-GH20 - Panzer Grenadier #2

HM-GH21 - German with 88mm Shell
HM-GH22 - SS Panzer Crewman
HM-GH25 - SS Officer in Camo

Recommended 1/35 heads with headdress

Hornet Models	HM-HGH01 German Caps
	HM-HGH02 German Fez
	HM-HGH03 German Camo
	HM-HGH04 German Helmets
	HM-HGH05 German Sidecaps
	HM-HGH08 German Officers
	HM-HGH11 German Peak Caps
	HM-HGH12 German Winter
	HM-HGH13 German Winter
	HM-HGH14 German Camo Caps
	HM-HGH17 WWII SS Sidecaps

Recommended 54mm figures

Andrea Miniatures	S5-F01 Leibstandarte SS 'Adolf Hitler'
	S5-F12 Mounted 'Florian Geyer' (1943)
	S5-F19 Waffen-SS Officer
	S5-F34 Waffen-SS Infantryman (1944)
	S5-F35 Obersturmführer (1945)
	S5-F39 German SS General (1942)
	S5-F40 German SS Officer (1936)
	S5-S03 Waffen SS MG42 Team
	S5-S07 Goose-Stepping Leibstandarte SS AH
Elisena	ELSN-10230 Sturmscharführer, Russia 1941

Recommended 120mm figures

Airborne Miniatures	AIRM-12036 Waffen SS, 1945
	AIRM-12039 SS Pioneer, WWII
	AIRM-12042 Totenkopf Gunner, 1945
	AIRM-12046 SS Radio Operator
	AIRM-12047 Waffen SS Pioneer
	AIRM-12051 German with Panzerfaust
	AIRM-903 NCO, SS Motorized Recon
S&T Products	ST-16007 SS Rotenfuhrer, Ardennes
	ST-16013 SS Tiger Crew, Kharkov
	ST-16014 SS Panzer Commander, Kharkov
	ST-16015 SS Panzer Crewman, Kharkov
	ST-16016 Panzer Grenadier, Kharkov
	ST-16018 Rotenfuhrer with MP40, Kharkov
	ST-16020 SS Sturmmann, 1944
	ST-16022 Grenadier, Kharkov
	ST-16026 Waffen SS, 1943
Miniature Alliance	SS Panzer Officer MA2012
Think 180 Studios	TOES-80001 SS Schutze, WWII

Retailers' websites

Colorado Miniatures	http://www.coloradominiatures.com/
Historex Agents	http://www.historexagents.com/ shop/hxshop.php
Hobby Link Japan	http://www.hlj.com/
Mission Models	http://www.missionmodels.com/
The M Workshop	http://themworkshop.com/
Chesapeake Model Designs	http://www.chesapeakemodels.com/
RMZ Imports	http://www.rzm.com/main/main.cfm

Further reading and research

Books

Beaver, Michael D.; *Uniform, SS Earth-grey Service Uniform, Model 1936 Field Service Uniform, 1939-1940, 1941*, vol. 1 (Schiffer Publishing)

Beaver, Michael D.; *Uniforms of the Waffen-SS: 1942, 1943, 1944–1945, Ski Uniforms, Overcoats, White Service Uniforms, Tropical Clothing*, vol. 2 (Schiffer Publishing)

Beaver, Michael D.; *Uniforms of the Waffen-SS: Sports and Drill Uniforms, Black Panzer Uniform, Camouflage, Concentration Camp Personnel, SD, SS Female Auxiliaries*, vol. 3 (Schiffer Publishing)

Beaver, Michael and Borsarello, J.F.; *Camouflage Uniforms of the Waffen SS: A Photographic Reference* (Schiffer Publishing)

Borsarello, J.F. and Lassus, Denis; *Camouflaged Uniforms of the Waffen SS* (ISO-Galago)

German Soldiers of World War Two (Histoire & Collections)

Michulec, Robert and Volstad, Ronald; *Waffen SS: (1) Forging an Army 1934–1943* (Concord Publications)

Michulec, Robert and Volstad, Ronald; *Waffen SS: (2) From glory to Defeat 1943–1945* (Concord Publications)

Michulec, Robert and Volstad, Ronald; *Waffen SS in Combat* (Concord Publications)

Nipe, George and Spezzano, Remy; *Platz Der Leibstandarte: A Photo Study of the SS-Panzer-Grenadier-Division Leibstandarte SS Adolf Hitler and the Battle for Kharkov January-March 1943* (RZM Publishing)

Pallud, Jean-Paul; Elite 11: *Ardennes 1944 Peiper & Skorzeny*

Peterson, Daniel; Europa Militaria Series: *Waffen-SS Camouflage Uniforms and Post-war Derivatives* (The Crowood Press)

Quarrie, Bruce; Warrior 2: *Waffen-SS Soldier 1940–45* (Osprey Publishing)

Spezzano, Remy; *Waffen SS Kursk: 1943* (RZM Publishing)

Steven, Andrew and Amodio, Peter; Europa Militaria, No. 6: *Waffen-SS Uniforms: In Colour Photographs* (The Crowood Press)

Terui, Yoshihiro; *Uniforms of the Waffen SS* (Dainippon-Kaiga)

Waffen-SS in the West: Holland, Belgium, France 1940 (Schiffer Publishing)

Walther, Herbert; *Waffen-SS* (Schiffer Publishing)

Windrow, Martin; Men-at-Arms 34: *The Waffen-SS* (Osprey Publishing)

Williamson, Gordon; Men-at-Arms 213: *German Military Police Units 1939–45* (Osprey Publishing)

Williamson, Gordon; Men-at-Arms 401: *The Waffen-SS (1) 1. to 5. Divisions* (Osprey Publishing)

Williamson, Gordon; Men-at-Arms 404: *The Waffen-SS (2) 6. to 10. Divisions* (Osprey Publishing)

Williamson, Gordon; Men-at-Arms 415: *The Waffen-SS (3) 11. to 23. Divisions* (Osprey Publishing)

Williamson, Gordon; Men-at-Arms 420: *The Waffen-SS (4) 24. to 38. Divisions, & Volunteer Legions* (Osprey Publishing)

Williamson, Gordon; Warrior 61: *German Security and Police Soldier 1939–45* (Osprey Publishing)

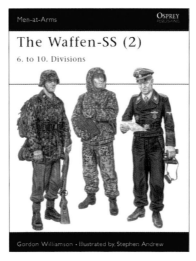

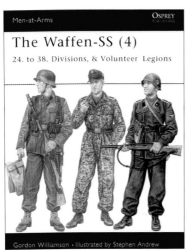

ABOVE LEFT Osprey Publishing's Men-at-Arms 401, *The Waffen-SS (1) 1. to 5. Divisions*

ABOVE MIDDLE Osprey Publishing's Men-at-Arms 404, *The Waffen-SS (2) 6. to 10. Divisions*

ABOVE RIGHT Osprey Publishing's Men-at-Arms 415, *The Waffen-SS (3) 11. to 23. Divisions*

FAR LEFT Osprey Publishing's Men-at-Arms 420, *The Waffen-SS (4) 24. to 38. Divisions & Volunteer Legions*

LEFT Osprey Publishing's Warrior 2, *Waffen-SS Soldier 1940–45*

Internet reference sites

STEINER	http://www2.neweb.ne.jp/wc/STEINER/
Collectors Guild	http://www.germanmilitaria.com/
1944 Militaria	http://www.1944militaria.com/
Thüringen Militaria	http://www.thuringenmilitaria.com/index.html
At the Front	http://www.atthefront.com/
G-Max	http://pacificcoast.net/~gmax/index.htm
Feldgrau.com	http://feldgrau.com/
Dunns Bunker	http://www.dunnsbunker.com/

Index